Seeing the Light

Gospel stories from the sidelines

Ruth Carter

O&U
Onwards & Upwards

Onwards and Upwards Publishers

4 The Old Smithy, London Road, Rockbeare,
EX5 2EA, United Kingdom.
www.onwardsandupwards.org

Copyright © Ruth Carter 2022

The right of Ruth Carter to be identified as the author of this work has been asserted by the author in accordance with the Copyright, Designs and Patents Act 1988.

All rights reserved.

No part of this publication may be reproduced or transmitted in any form or by any means, electronic or mechanical, including photocopy, recording or any information storage and retrieval system, without permission in writing from the author or publisher.

First edition, published in the United Kingdom by Onwards and Upwards Publishers (2022).

ISBN: 978-1-78815-985-2
Typeface: Sabon LT

The views and opinions expressed in this book are the author's own, and do not necessarily represent the views and opinions of Onwards and Upwards Publishers or its staff.

Where exactly quoted, Scripture quotations are taken from the Holy Bible, New International Version® Anglicized, NIV® Copyright © 1979, 1984, 2011 by Biblica, Inc.® Used by permission. All rights reserved worldwide. Other Scripture quotations have been paraphrased by the author.

Endorsements

How do we create a feeling of surprise about Christianity in a society that views all religion with suspicion, is allergic to dogma but hungers after spirituality? Ruth Carter responds to this challenge by enabling a new generation of readers to meet Jesus through an imaginative retelling of the encounters and experiences of different characters in the Gospel. Her writing is fresh and accessible, bringing situations and people to life, and allowing us to find our place in the story and to 'see the light'.

Rt Revd Robert Atwell
Bishop of Exeter

Using a conversational style, Ruth invites the reader to meet with some of the 'smaller' characters in the Gospels. Her imaginative approach to the Gospel narrative brings these individuals to life in a new way and encourages us to enter into their story. As we do so, we are invited to make connections between these individual stories and the wider biblical metanarrative by the helpful biblical quotes used by the author. Whether you are exploring the Scriptures for the first time or are more familiar with the text, this book will help you to deepen your own journey of faith.

Revd Ann Coleman
Co-ordinator, Chelmsford diocese spiritual direction network

Ruth Carter's retellings of Gospel stories are luminous. With compelling imagination and vivid prose, she takes us into the lives, concerns and hopes of the women and men who encountered Jesus. The settings are deftly realised, the characters' voices thoroughly believable, but deeper than all that is Carter's capturing of moments of transformation. Again and again, she leads us to the point in the story where light breaks through, and life is illuminated. The gift of this beautiful book is its transparency to that light.

Prof. Mike Higton
Professor of Theology and Ministry, Durham University

Seeing the Light

Contents

Foreword 7
1. A New Dawn 9
2. The Sign of a Prophet 13
3. The Kingdom of God 17
4. An Invitation to Dinner 21
5. Light in the Darkness 25
6. Counting the Cost 29
7. Cementing Power 33
8. A Day to Remember 37
9. Crossing Boundaries 41
10. Parting of the Ways 45
11. Peter Climbs a Mountain 49
12. Family Tensions 53
13. The Price of Success 58
14. Who Rules Israel? 62
15. Telling the Truth 66
16. A Terrible Mistake 70
17. The Light Returns 73
18. God With Us 77

Seeing the Light

Foreword

I can't really remember a time when I didn't know stories from the Gospels. They formed part of my cultural background, as unquestioned and comfortable as fairy tales. Training as a lay preacher much later in life, I noticed how easily my attention slipped over the surface of such familiar stories. Like stones worn smooth by years of passing feet, they provided no grip. I wanted to try to get some purchase on the stories again, to rediscover for myself (and perhaps pass on to others) their challenge and power. So I began experimenting with narrative sermons, trying to reimagine what it might have been like for those who heard the words of Jesus for the first time, not knowing anything about the end of his story or the church doctrine that would be built on it. Encounters in the Gospels are regularly marked with a mixture of faith and perplexity. Some people have startling insights, but others miss the point entirely. Those closest to Jesus often need to have teachings repeated and explained before they get the message. But almost no one seems to react to him with indifference.

In retelling these stories from the perspective of other participants, I wanted to discover a sense of how extraordinary it would be to come face to face with God without knowing it. As far as possible, I have tried to use the dialogue reported in the Gospels, and historically accurate background information, but of course I have had to invent all sorts of details to flesh out the characters. To that extent this is a work of fiction. All my narrators are unreliable in the sense that they don't know how the story will end. Even those with most insight only partially understand who Jesus is, and they all bring their own prejudices to their version of events. But I hope that through their misunderstandings and questions, they make space for each of us to explore our own experience of God.

1

A New Dawn

The Presentation in the Temple

by Anna

LUKE 2:22-40

Some people hate being old. I prefer to think of it as a privilege. After all, what's the alternative? I remember my husband, dead at twenty-eight when a barn wall collapsed. Wouldn't he rather be here now, whatever the state of his joints? Of course it's not easy, but when has life ever been that? I was lucky; I was taken in by my in-laws, for the sake of the grandsons I'd borne to them, but mainly for my free labour. Their old age was eased by my service; I was kept busy milling, baking, weaving, cleaning and endlessly fetching water. I can still feel the ache of it in my back. But really, it wasn't such a bad life. The old people were never cruel to me, even if they took me for granted. They knew, as I did, that without them I would be destitute. And to be truthful, when they came to die, I felt cast adrift, as lost as my tribe when they were cut off from Israel so many centuries ago, even though I live in the heart of Jerusalem. What was my role now? My children were grown and married, making their own lives, raising the new generation. My son gave me a home, for which I must be grateful, but not a purpose.

I don't remember when I started to visit the temple. I do know that I very quickly found it a place of sanctuary, where I could escape my daughter-in-law's piercing voice and where an old woman could pass time in peace, with no one to question her motives. I don't think I was very devout. I just enjoyed the sense of being a still point in the bustle. I watched all the busy people coming and going, the priests with their robes and self-importance, the temple guard, all uniforms and bravado, the throng of anxious petitioners, bringing their offerings and seeking guidance before hurrying off again to pick up their lives outside.

Over time I became such a familiar figure that the officials stopped even noticing me. I was part of the scenery, indistinguishable from the stonework. But strangely, as I grew invisible to human eyes, I started to feel as if I was becoming visible to God – or, should that be, *God* started to become visible to *me*? I don't mean I saw visions; it was something more shadowy than that. Slowly, as I adjusted to the rhythm of the temple seasons, I began to be aware of the threads of a message that whispered through the courts.

Now I sound like a mad old bat. Perhaps I am – certainly no one took any notice of what I had to say. There's not much call for women's voices these days. Once upon a time, they say, women were prophets and even rulers: Deborah and Huldah, and those unnamed wise women the ancient kings consulted when they were at their wits' end. Today, if you know what's good for you, you keep your head down and bow submissively, even if you can see someone's making a mistake. It's fine to have an opinion on household matters, but as soon as you step outdoors – or worse, don't have a home to run at all – you're a threat to the established order. If you ask me (and, of course, no one does) I think it's got worse since the Romans came. Their wives are very definitely of the seen-and-not-heard variety, and anyone who wants to get on in Jerusalem these days has to show how Roman they are. So there's a general feeling that women belong at home, and if they do go out in public they should remember their place.

Well, that's fine by me. I learnt quickly that my husband's family weren't interested in my opinions, and nor is my daughter-in-law. In any case, the ideas that filled my head in the temple seemed like a secret, something just for me. I began spending more time in the women's courtyard, waiting to see if more thoughts would come. As the sounds of the priests singing their prayers floated out of the inner court, I found myself listening to their words. And when the priests weren't around I made up my own prayers. *"Lord, Holy One of Israel, come and heal your people."* I thought of the people I saw day after day flocking through the entrance gates: busy, preoccupied and purposeful. From my place in the shadows, I started to notice things about them, the telltale anxiety of people with a place to maintain in society; the exhausted faces of the poor; the sagging shoulders of the bereaved. So much longing, so much pain.

Once I'd started seeing it, I couldn't stop. Some days I felt flooded with pity, unmoored, adrift on a sea of human need. My only lifeline was that voice in my head, God's voice: *"Do not fear, Israel, for I have redeemed you; I have summoned you by name; you are mine."*

At home the memory of the people followed me, but the voice didn't. It was only in the temple that I found its reassurance. Even there, sometimes weeks passed and I heard nothing, only the lapping ocean of suffering. I didn't know what to do with it except to hold it out to God, a sort of challenge: *"You say you care for us, but look at these people: what are you doing for them?"*

I wondered if I'd be struck dead for such presumption. My husband would certainly have slapped me for it. But God, it turned out, was kinder than my husband. Words formed in my head, the language of half-remembered readings from Scripture, potent with a new meaning. "I am about to do a new thing; now it springs forth, do you not perceive it?"

One day, I saw a woman weeping in the courtyard and couldn't bear to see her alone. I went to stand alongside her, just to give her the gift of company. But she looked at me with such emptiness that I had to speak.

"The Lord is coming," I whispered. "He will redeem Jerusalem. He brings a new thing."

A tiny flame of hope rose in her eyes. And just like that, I found what I had to do. Quietly, without drawing attention to myself, I passed on the words that came to me. I came to recognise those who were ready to hear them, whose loneliness or sorrow or gratitude opened their ears and hearts. And all the while I kept watching for what God's new thing would be.

Today a family group passed me on their way into the inner courtyard: a young mother, with a baby in her arms, and a father gripping two struggling pigeons. They were clearly poor, but they had that glow of hope that firstborn babies sometimes bring. There's something luminous about a new life, the endless possibilities contained in that tiny person. I might be old, but you mustn't think I've forgotten what a miracle it is when a child is born. Seeing this one, my heart lifted suddenly, a blessed relief from the weight of so much pain. The family disappeared through the inner gate and I found myself hoping I'd see them on the way out.

They were a long time inside – perhaps there was some delay in performing the sacrifice – but eventually they reappeared, heading back down the steps towards the outside world. The mother looked grave, and the father had a protective arm around her. What had happened to blot out their joy? I wished I could rekindle their youthful enthusiasm. Heaven knows, there's little enough of that in this world.

"May I see the child?" I asked.

The mother was resigned but polite. She handed me the bundle with that infinite care that young parents have, before they have forgotten how precious a new life is. But when I held their baby in my arms, I understood she wasn't just an inexperienced mother. The child blazed with life, like a distillation of every dream and hope and possibility that has ever been. It was as if I held the sun itself in my hands. I heard the voice of God as I'd never heard it before. *"Behold, I make all things new."* I had thought I might offer some words of comfort to the parents, but what I found myself saying was, "God be praised, for his salvation has come to us!"

The mother's eyes met mine then, and I looked at her in awe. I sometimes feel overwhelmed bringing the needs of the world to God. What an unimaginable responsibility must it be to bring the light of God into the world?

It was the briefest of encounters, but hours later, my mind is still full of that little family: the brave, determined father; the mother who understands already that the price of love is pain; and the extraordinary baby, almost weightless in my arms, who somehow lifted all the weight of a city's cares from my heart. In its place is a joy I had forgotten how to feel, and a new message for those who come to the temple courts: *the day of our redemption has dawned.*

2

The Sign of a Prophet

The Baptism of Jesus
by a follower of John

LUKE 3:1-22

Believe me, it's a long way to the Jordan river: a slow, dusty road, with the relentless heat making each mile feel longer than the one before. Setting off, we were full of hope and fervour. Somewhere in the fifth hour, hot, dirty and footsore, I wondered what had possessed me. But then the road crested a hill and we could see the shimmer of the water in the valley below, snaking through a green ribbon of foliage, glinting in the heat. All I could think was how blissful it would be to plunge into that cool water. I forgot for a moment that the object of our journey was a person, not a bath.

To understand why we went, you have to remember that things have been getting more and more uncomfortable in Judaea. With every passing year the pressure builds up a little, until it's simmering on the edge of revolt. When you're turned off land that your family has farmed for generations so an occupying army can build a road, the sting of that doesn't go away. When they replace your king with a foreign governor, who barely speaks your language and cares even less about your way of life, you know you were right not to trust their promises of peace. When the dirty collaborators who collect taxes for the Romans demand more every year, making themselves rich on the proceeds while honest families starve, is it surprising that tensions start to rise? People have started to ask if God has deserted us. How can Israel's protector allow us to be enslaved on our own soil? And if God abandons us, who will rescue us?

In the old days, the stories say, there were prophets, wild men with untameable messages of destruction, vengeance and glory. They pointed God's people back to the right path, filling them with courage for battle and wisdom for life. They were larger than life, characters to fill your mind with wonder and strengthen your resolve: Elijah calling down fire from heaven; Samuel seeking out and anointing great King David when he was nothing but a scrawny shepherd boy; Isaiah the visionary who looked into the face of God himself. But there are no prophets now; only rabbis poring over the scrolls to tease out their meaning, and a high priest in Jerusalem who does what the Romans tell him. So when we heard there was a preacher by the Jordan with a message of renewal, a man of the wilderness with fire in his eyes, it felt like a flicker of hope for our nation. The least we could do was go and see for ourselves.

It turned out we weren't the only ones. As we approached the river, we met throngs of people heading the same way, arguing about who or what they'd come to see. A leader, said some. A rabbi, said others. A prophet was what we were hoping for, someone to point the way to a better future.

We heard him before we saw him. He was haranguing the crowd, telling them everything that they'd done wrong, no holds barred. There was something thrilling about the passion in his voice. You could tell straight away, this was a man who wouldn't compromise. He'd go to his death shouting about the truth. And he didn't care who he offended along the way. Instead of sweet-talking the crowd, he insulted them. He threatened them with destruction, decapitation and wildfire. When someone reminded him of our birthright as Abraham's children, he laughed.

"Don't count on it," he said. "The stones under your feet are better children to Abraham than you've ever been. You've broken the covenant. Why should God keep faith with you? Can't you see your days are numbered?"

People looked uneasy at that. Preaching renewal is all very well, but they hadn't counted on being denounced to their faces.

"What should we do?" someone asked.

Then he really got into his stride. I'll say this for him, he wasn't just a doom-monger. He had practical ideas. *Get down in the river and wash away your sins. Then start again. Share what you have, don't be greedy, don't use your power for your own benefit.* He didn't take sides. Ordinary people, tax collectors on the take, even a group of off-duty soldiers – he had an answer for everyone. To be honest, I wasn't too comfortable being lumped together with the appeasers and the collaborators. But it did make me wonder if perhaps we spend too much energy on denouncing each other. Maybe the preacher was right, that we've all failed in one way or another, and we all need to change our ways.

As the crowd jostled around him, I finally got a proper view. The Baptiser, they called him. If he wanted to be taken for a prophet, he certainly looked the part: unkempt, wild-eyed and dressed in camel hair – just like Elijah in the Desert of Damascus. People were starting to whisper: *Is this the Messiah? Will he be the one to rescue Israel?* Even I felt my heart beat faster. Could it be?

It was as if he'd overheard my thoughts. "Don't look at me. I'm just the forerunner. I'm here to prepare the way. The one you're waiting for is so far above me, I'm not even worthy to loosen his shoe. But you lot – I'll give you a bath if that's what you're here for!"

By now, the crowd would have jumped off a cliff if he'd told them to. So one by one, we waded into the river, the credulous, the sceptical and the curious. The Baptiser was waiting in mid-stream, and he ducked us under the water. He must have said some words over me, but they were drowned out by the noise of the water in my ears. I stood up, spluttering and wiping the water from my face. Did I feel new? Not very, if I'm honest – but I did have that tingle of hope again. Here were hundreds of people who wanted change, and – at least for that brief moment – we were fired up to begin by changing ourselves. We were enlisted in God's service and we belonged together. Maybe, just maybe, this would be the start of a movement that would make a difference.

I'd barely scrambled back on to the bank when there was a commotion among the crowd. Past the pointing fingers I saw a man standing chest-deep in the river, as motionless as if he were on solid ground, his head bowed. I can't really describe what happened next. It was as if everything – the trees, the air, the water – was reaching towards him, the way an eddy in a stream pulls in floating leaves to its path. He lifted his face to the heavens, and at that moment the clouds parted, bathing him in a brilliant light. From somewhere high above came a bird, a dove, seemingly drawn by the same force towards the silent man. He never flinched as it hovered right over him, brushing his head with its wings. Then there was a rumble of thunder like the voice of heaven – and the bird was gone. But what an omen! The sign of Noah, the dove flying over the waters, bringing news of salvation.

All of a sudden I knew, as surely as if I had heard the words spoken, that this man would be special. He didn't look it. He seemed quite normal

– neither old nor young, muscled from manual work, not rich but not destitute; one of us. But what happened in the river meant something, I'm sure of it.

I came hoping to see a prophet – and the Baptiser was certainly fiery enough. With his intensity, his uncompromising message and his sheer, brutal charisma, he could have been a leader to give the Romans pause for thought. But he wanted to stir up our blood for something – or *someone* – else. He was like the rest of us in that; he was waiting in the dark, except that he'd realised that part of the waiting is preparing. If we want God to help us, we have to live by his laws of justice and care for others, not mimic the invaders with their cruelty and their insatiable greed for money, territory and control. *Return to God and he will return to you* – that's always been the message of the prophets.

If I'm honest, I'd hoped for something flashier – a sign from heaven, not just words and water. But turning it over in my mind now, I keep remembering the other man, the one the dove flew over. He didn't act like a prophet. He didn't say anything at all, and after the business with the thunder he vanished back into the crowd. But I can't shake the feeling that there was more to that moment than we could see. Perhaps the signs of the prophets were there after all. As I replay the scene in my memory, the dove hovering over him might almost have been anointing him, the way Samuel anointed David. That shaft of sunlight was like Elijah's fire coming down from heaven. And the brightness of it on his face made him look as if he, like Isaiah, had seen the face of God and lived.

3

The Kingdom of God

Healing a Demoniac

by a bystander

LUKE 11:14-28

Well, that really wasn't what I expected to see in the market today. I was just going about my business (the usual errands, hoping to bump into a friend and catch up on some of the news, maybe – just a normal day), when I saw a crowd gathering near the well. So of course I wandered over to have a look. Not much happens in this town at the best of times and it might make a story to tell over dinner. The crowd was gathered around the tree where the man who can't speak sits. Normally we all give him a wide berth; it's not as if he's very good company. To be honest he gives me the creeps, with his animal grunts and waving hands. People say there's a demon living in him, and you don't want to get too close to demons; who knows what might happen? So we all avoid the man who can't speak. I suppose he has a pretty lonely time of it. Not much of a life, really.

Today, though, he was right at the centre of the action. When I got closer, I could see that he looked somehow different – sitting still, instead of flailing around and doing that weird thing with his tongue. He was staring up at a man beside him, as if he'd seen a ghost or something. There was lots of noise from the crowd, everyone trying to tell each other what had happened, then someone said, "He's trying to speak!" and there was a sudden silence.

So we all heard him.

This man, who I swear has not spoken a word in all the twenty years I've been coming here, he said, "Blessed is the one who comes in the name of the Lord." His voice sounded a bit hoarse, like a rusty wheel that's been out of action for too long, but the words were clear enough.

Seeing the Light

Well, then it all went a bit crazy. Everyone was shouting at once, some trying to get him to speak again, some yelling to their friends to come and look, but most of them were asking the healer guy what he was up to. We've seen his type before, of course – travelling sorcerers who turn up with cheap tricks to con people out of their money. Except usually they bring their sidekicks with them: fake cripples twisted into contorted shapes for show, who miraculously stand up straight; old men with milk smeared over their eyes to make them look blind, when they can see as well as I can. But this time was different – we all knew the man who couldn't speak, so he obviously wasn't in on the act. He looked as surprised as the rest of us.

"It's a demon!" said someone. "He's got a demon himself and that's how he got rid of this other one!"

That put the wind up me. Had this man just brought a bigger demon, and was he going to infect the whole town?

"Not just any old demon – the *prince* of demons!" said someone else.

A wave of fear ran through the crowd. Someone picked up a stone and looked as if he might be about to throw it.

"Oi, mate," shouted another, "show us a sign from God, if that's who sent you!"

The man just stood there, waiting. He didn't look like a messenger from God. He didn't look possessed, either, for that matter. But demons can be cunning. I started to edge away. Then he spoke, quietly, but in a voice that carried. There was something about him that made you want to listen to what he said, like the best storytellers. And not just listen, but believe what he told you. It sounds fanciful, but it seemed to me as if just the sound of his voice changed the whole atmosphere. In minutes, all that buzzing anxiety and aggression faded out, like when the wind drops after a storm.

I can't tell you exactly what he said. It all made perfect sense, and somehow, without once raising his voice, he cut through the confusion and accusations. He made us see that he couldn't be a demon, because that would mean the kingdom of demons was falling apart. (And wouldn't we all love to see that day!) Then he talked about a power stronger than the demons, stronger than the sorcerers and magicians who claim to control them, another kingdom but belonging to God. He said the kingdom had come to us – almost as if he had brought it. (But isn't Israel already God's kingdom? We're supposed to be his chosen people, although it doesn't feel like it most of the time. Anyway, he certainly wasn't behaving like any kind of royal ambassador. He looked more like a travelling tradesman to me. You could tell he'd done manual work. And his feet were filthy.) But the way he talked sounded like the heroic stories from the past, when King David went to war against the Canaanites and no one could stand against him. There was something stirring and triumphant about his words. He made us feel the glory days were back, that we could once again be on the winning side, not just reclaiming our country but restoring ourselves as well; that weakness and shame could be a thing of the past. I'm no fighter, but for a moment there I wanted to get in line behind him, and follow him into battle if need be.

You could tell the others were amazed by what he said, too. I've never seen a crowd hanging on someone's words like that. (Later, of course, when he'd gone, the arguments started up again. "He said we should rise up against the Romans!" "No, he said seven evil spirits are coming and we all need to lock down our houses and protect ourselves.")

But what stuck in my mind was a woman, right at the back, who shouted out, "She was a lucky woman, your mother, to feed you from her own breast!" I'm sure she meant well, but as soon as the words were out of her mouth you could tell she regretted them. No one trying to win over a crowd wants to be reminded of being a defenceless baby. I thought he might cut her down to size, like he did with the ones who said he was possessed, or maybe just ignore her. She was only a woman, after all. But he didn't do either.

He looked right at her, and I had the oddest feeling that he was thinking of his mother; his eyes had such kindness and respect in them. So when he disagreed with her, it didn't seem like a put-down, more like an invitation.

"The lucky ones are those who hear God's call, and obey it," he said. As if just anyone can join God's kingdom. As if even the unwanted and useless and socially clumsy have a part to play in this battle. As if all we have to do is listen to the truth and let it heal us; and then we'll become part of the movement that defeats the demons and makes the world a place worth living in again.

It all seemed so clear then. When this preacher, or prophet, or whatever he was, stood in the middle of us in the marketplace, he could have called us to march on the Roman garrison and we would have gone with him. But he didn't do that. He just sort of... slipped away. And life carried on and it was just an ordinary day after all. Except now the man who couldn't speak has found a voice. And there's still that thought: *I think he invited me to join God's kingdom.*

4

An Invitation to Dinner

The Anointing of Jesus
by Simon the Pharisee

LUKE 7:36-50

It was always a risk, inviting Jesus of Nazareth to dinner. There are plenty who believe he's a dangerous radical, undermining authority and stirring up the common people, destroying the delicate balance of politics and religion in this crowded country. Whether you like the Romans or loathe them, cooperation is vital to our survival, and the one thing they absolutely won't tolerate is any hint of insurrection. As long as the religious bodies maintain order, they allow us our freedom to follow the Law, keeping their disgusting idols at arm's length. But at the first hint of trouble, all their professed tolerance goes out of the window. Look at what's happened in Judaea: they got tired of the king and installed their own prefect in his place. What further sign is needed that we have failed to keep our covenant with God?

You only have to look at our history: all the golden promises of our own land, of freedom to fulfil our destiny as God's chosen race; and all the stories of disappointment, exile and enslavement. But the answers are there too: God's commandments written clearly for us to follow. If only we did! Why will people not open their eyes to the truth? We can't expect God to honour us, if we don't honour God. When we defile ourselves by living like heathens, of course the Holy One turns his face away. But there is a way back. It's not easy; it requires discipline and dedication, but surely the hope of our nation is worth a little sacrifice. When we call on God to deliver us from our oppressors, we have to remember our side of the bargain too.

That's where the Nazarene comes in. Although he has some very odd ideas, he does preach keeping the commandments. He calls people to righteousness and he certainly knows the Law. When he's questioned he always has a sound, scriptural answer for everything. Some would say he's a bit too clever – and he could definitely do with learning how to respect his elders. Still, there was always the hope that he might be drawn into our orbit, with a bit of encouragement. He certainly has the common touch; how wonderful if we could enlist him to spread the word among the labourers and craftsmen! It might be our route to a mass movement, a new commitment of the people to the Law.

It was too good an opportunity to pass up. So I sent him an invitation to dinner, which he properly turned down (showing he knows how etiquette works, even if he mostly chooses to ignore it). I invited him a second time and he agreed. That wasn't a surprise; what man would ignore the chance to mix with his social superiors? I'm willing to bet I serve better food than he's seen in a while, too. The other guests were members of my circle, although it's true some were reluctant to accept. Several were worried that his very presence would defile them. I had to reassure them that he would be seated in the lowest place, so there was no danger he'd be dipping his bread into the same bowl.

He was late to arrive, which did surprise me; I can't think what better things he had to do. By the time he turned up, the party was in full swing and the servants were busy fetching drinks and titbits for the other guests. The doorman wasn't paying attention and failed to warn me, so the first I knew of his arrival was when he appeared in the dining room. It was an awkward moment, which I'd hoped to get out of the way in private. Should I greet him as an equal, with a kiss on both cheeks? But I couldn't be sure he'd made the correct preparations, so that risked making me unclean. On the other hand, I couldn't *not* acknowledge the arrival of an invited guest. I gave him a small nod (not so deep that anyone could think I was blaspheming by bowing down to him) and gestured to his seat. Then I called for the food to be brought in.

I'd had two hopes for the evening. The first was that the Nazarene would spell out his teaching so that we could make a better judgement of his position. Was he a potential ally, just in need of some guidance to rein in his more extreme positions? Or was he as dangerous as they said? The other (more remote, admittedly) was that being at a meal with his betters would open his eyes to the advantages of joining us. I've always believed that you shouldn't make enemies where there's a chance of making friends. It was worth showing a bit of charity if it could avoid conflict later.

Things began quite well. For a carpenter, he was surprisingly at ease in polite company, and if he argued, he always spoke respectfully of the Scriptures and of the rabbis. My friends started to relax, and the conversation flowed freely. Then all at once I became aware of an interruption. There had been people coming and going throughout the meal, clients of one or other of the guests, and various hangers-on hoping for scraps. I barely noticed them until someone nudged me and pointed to the bottom of the table where the Nazarene was reclining. A woman we all recognised, a common prostitute, was bending over his feet, weeping.

"This should be interesting," whispered my friend. "If he's a prophet, he'll know what she is."

But the Nazarene showed no sign of disgust. Then, unbelievably, the whore undid her hair and used it to try to wipe up the mess. Prophet or not, if he had any sense of propriety he'd have reacted to that. No respectable woman lets her hair down in public, and she certainly wouldn't touch a man she's never met. As we watched, horrified, she broke her perfume jar, massaged the ointment into his feet and kissed them.

The whole scene was beyond embarrassing. My friends looked to me to put a stop to it. But before I could say anything, the Nazarene spoke up.

"Simon," he said, "I've got a story for you."

"Tell me, Teacher," I answered, barely managing to keep the sarcasm out of my voice. A man who lets a prostitute defile him in public has nothing to teach me.

It was one of his odd little stories, about debts and forgiveness. There was a question at the end, but the answer he wanted was obvious: of course, the bigger debtor is the more grateful. I assumed he was trying to divert attention from the woman still messing around with his feet. But then he referred to her directly, contrasting her with me in the most insulting way possible. *The arrogance of the man!* Did he not understand the honour that I'd bestowed on him just by inviting him into my house? If he turned up too late to have the servants attend to his feet, was that my fault?

It's a host's duty to be courteous, even in the face of extreme rudeness, so I resisted the urge to have him whipped and thrown out. It was clear by then that my strategy had failed; there was no future in trying to cooperate with this man. We could have lived with his rough manners, but his defiance in the face of the most basic purity laws made it clear that he was not interested in an obedient relationship with God. And that was before he made his most outrageous claim: telling the woman that her sins were forgiven. If he knows his Scriptures as he pretends to, he must know that only the Almighty can forgive sins. I see now what he's doing: buying support among the vulnerable and uneducated by pretending that there's an easy way to God's favour – and he can provide it. But the Law teaches us that God's mercy is bestowed on those who keep his commandments. If we serve God well and faithfully, he will forgive the sins we and others have committed, and show us his love. The Nazarene has turned that on its head; in *his* topsy-turvy world, God starts by forgiving us, we respond by loving him and that inspires us to a life of gratitude and service.

It's an appealing vision, but it can't be right. It would mean a complete redesigning of the covenant between God and his people, overturning centuries of tradition. Where would all our efforts to keep the Law be, if God's love is there for the asking? What's the point of all the sacrifices we've made, if God accepts us anyway? And without the fear of judgement, what incentive would anyone have to follow God's path? The Nazarene might have convinced the common people, but he doesn't understand the heart of true religion. If you ask me, it won't be long before he's discredited, and then his movement will just fizzle out. Only God's truth can stand the test of time.

5

Light in the Darkness

Jesus Heals a Haemorrhage
by the woman with the flow of blood

MARK 5:24-34

Can you imagine what it's like to be a prisoner in your own house, sealed up like a corpse in a tomb, not for a week, or a month or a year, but for a decade and more? What would be left of you, when activity and friendship and hope have shrivelled away? That has been my world for twelve years; while my friends have raised their families, life has passed me by and the future has slipped through my hands. Once upon a time I was a new bride, glowing with possibility and full of dreams. I would keep house for my husband, bear him children and raise them to be a tribute to us both. I was young and strong, new to womanhood but well-schooled by my mother and sisters in what to expect from married life. Yet they never told me about the pain; and no one had any idea what to do when the bleeding started – *and wouldn't stop*. Everyone agrees it's not my husband's fault. The rot comes from inside me – as if my body's trying to expel its own life.

To start with, everyone was very kind. They made me rest, assuming time would heal me. Then came the time of the doctors, each one with a cure worse than the last – foul-tasting concoctions which made me vomit and spasm; compresses; baths; special diets. Nothing worked. The bleeding went on and on, and the pain made me dizzy. By then, people had started to keep their distance. The rabbis tell us blood is the source of life itself, but blood that trickles out of your body makes you unclean. A woman has to keep herself apart when she's bleeding so that she doesn't pollute others. My husband started to sleep on the floor; at first he said it was to give me chance to rest, but soon it became a habit. He was always gentle with me, but I could feel the frustration behind his mildness. What good is a wife with a broken, leaking body? How can she bear a child if her own life force is always leaking away? When he told me he was going to marry again, it was almost a relief. My dowry was gone; there was no more money for doctors. "It's in the hands of God now," he said. He made me some living space in an old animal shed in our compound. At least there I could live in peace, not scurrying to hide every time anyone came near.

But I watched as his new wife blossomed and swelled, and their children were born, and thrived, and I thought of the children that should have been mine, washed away in the red tide. Sometimes it would pause for days or weeks on end, and then I'd hope that some miracle had cured me, but sooner or later it always began again. Alone indoors, with only my thoughts for company, I wondered how my body could keep going. How was I still alive, losing all this blood? What never-failing source kept replenishing my veins? And there was another, darker question: *why?* Back in the days of treatments, we went to the rabbi and asked his advice. Was God angry with me? He told me to think back over my life and examine my conscience. What sin had I committed to provoke God's wrath? Well, in all the empty days and lonely nights I had plenty of time to ask that question, and truthfully I couldn't come up with anything that might have merited such harsh punishment. Of course I've done things I shouldn't, but no worse than others I know. Still, I begged God's forgiveness, and begged him to show me where I'd gone wrong. In my head I went over and over the words of the Scriptures I remembered from visits to the synagogue. Perhaps one of them would show me where I was at fault.

As months passed, and my days dissolved to inactivity and my opportunities for sinning all but disappeared, I found it harder to believe that I could be responsible for God's continued displeasure. Instead I found my mind returning to the words of a psalm like a refrain: "The Lord is my shepherd, who gives me all I need. He will feed me and house me, and guide me even through the valley of the shadow of death." Living in this dim room, the valley of the shadow sounded an apt description. Death, though, seemed to have forgotten me. All I was left with was the hope that the shepherd God might one day hear my prayer and lead me out of my captivity. Didn't he do that once for our people?

When my sister slipped into my room one day, with a basket of figs and some news to tell, her enthusiasm grated against my hard-won resignation. "Have you heard?" she said breathlessly. "There's a miracle-worker in town! He's travelling round the region healing people, even those born sick. You must hurry to see him before he moves on." She was so hopeful that it seemed cruel to tell her how ridiculous her idea was. If I displayed myself in public like that, someone would be bound to recognise my face and denounce me for defiling them all. I'd be lucky to escape without a stoning. "Go on," urged my sister; "you won't be seen in the crowd. He's always surrounded by flocks of people – maybe that's why they call him the shepherd."

Well, perhaps that word was a sign. I suddenly felt weary of watching my life ebb away. I put on my cloak and pulled the hood over my face so no one would know me. With my sister's help I crept out of the compound and followed her the few short streets to the marketplace. The crowd was so dense it was easy to pass unnoticed, and we were swept on towards the synagogue. It was strange to be among people again; they moved almost like a river, eddying and surging in unseen currents. Suddenly we came out of a side street and there was the healer, right in front of us. He had a gang of men round him, trying to protect him from the jostling crowd, but they all had their backs to us. *What if I just touch his robe?* I thought. *Then he won't even need to know I've come near him, and I can slip away unnoticed.* I bent under the reaching arms of the crowd and stretched out my hand, praying I wouldn't fall and be trampled on.

I don't know what I thought would happen, but this was like nothing I could have imagined. As my fingers grasped at the fringe of his robe, I felt as if a shaft of sunlight had fallen on me, intense enough to make me catch my breath, and yet gentle and warm. It lit up all the dark recesses of my thoughts as clear as midday – all my fears and bitterness, all the festering pain – and bathed them in a soft, liquid light that washed me clean. For a moment, time stood still. I felt the familiar tingling and dizziness and thought I was going to faint, but as my head cleared I was overtaken with a certainty that something in me had changed; the bleeding was gone. I was so astonished, I forgot where I was – and then someone shoved me sideways into the path of the oncoming crowd. I scrambled to reach the edge of the street, hoping to slip away, but the healer had stopped.

"Who touched me?" he asked. I could see the bodyguards looking perplexed: dozens of people were pressing against him. He turned round and scanned the crowd. "I felt power go out of me," he said, and his eyes fell on me, even as I shrank back against the wall.

I knew I'd had it then. Everyone was looking at me. The crowd would turn on me the moment they realised who I was. And the healer would be furious with me for making him unclean. The bodyguards looked as if they'd be handy with a stone or two. But there was no escape. I stumbled towards him, as people drew back to let me through. My legs didn't seem to be working any more, so I knelt at his feet. He bent down towards me.

"Don't touch me; I'm unclean," I whispered. "I'm bleeding—" and then I stopped. "I've been bleeding for twelve years and no one could heal me. But you healed me." When I dared to look up, his eyes were deep and cool, like pools of still water. His hand rested for a moment on my shoulder, as if in blessing. "Daughter," he said, "your faith has healed you. Go and find peace."

Even now I don't know what he meant by that. My *faith?* I didn't feel as if I had any faith left, after all those years of failed treatments and unanswered prayers. I had a moment of madness brought on by my sister's excitement, and a sudden longing to break free of my prison. And I had a few words from a psalm that took root in my brain and wouldn't let go, and the chance coincidence of a healer's nickname.

He's gone now, to gather another flock in another village, but I will always think of him as my good shepherd, who brought me out of the valley of shadow into the sunlit pastures, who restored my body to health, and gave me back my place in the community. I didn't imagine it: the bleeding has gone. The doctors have confirmed it and the priest has pronounced me clean. There's no way to restore the years that have passed, and I grieve for the chances that will not come my way again. But now I am finally free to go in and out as I choose, to feel the sun on my skin, and to wonder at the memory of that moment, when the hem of a stranger's robe seemed to contain within it all the light of the world.

6

Counting the Cost

Jesus Raises a Girl from the Dead
by Jairus

MARK 5:21-24,35-43

What's the most important thing in life? A week ago, I would have said a man's place in society. If you have status, everything else follows: friends, influence, and the opportunity to turn things to your advantage, from business deals to marriage contracts. Believe me, I know what I'm talking about. I have achieved all of those things. Ruler of the synagogue, prominent landowner, wife from the best local family. If I had any sense of regret, it might have been that we only had the one surviving child, but that was more my wife's concern than mine. I had plenty else to worry about. It's true that we weren't getting any younger, but there was still always hope that more children might come along. How much attention does a man pay to a daughter anyway? Not enough, in my case. I took her for granted – her brightness and laughter, her searching questions and her easy innocence, the quiet peace of her body when she slept.

She's never been a sickly child, so when my wife sent word she had contracted a fever I didn't pay much attention at first. Then another message came – "Come at once, we're losing her!" – and immediately I felt a terrible foreboding. I dropped what I was doing and ran, while the synagogue officials stared. At home the door was shaded and there was a strange hush over that normally busy house. I knew then that my daughter was dying, and all I could do was kneel at her bedside as the light of the future was extinguished before my eyes. I held her hand and begged her to stay with us, and when she couldn't answer me I begged God to spare her life. It wasn't right; she was just a child. How could God be asking this of her? How could God be asking this of me?

29

Unwanted, the story of Abraham came into my head. God asked for Abraham's son and Abraham offered him gladly, taking a knife to his own child's throat. Hearing that story in the synagogue, my heart would swell with pride for the faith of our ancestor who gave up his future for God, trusting in God's promise regardless of appearances. I'd listened and nodded when the rabbis encouraged us to follow Abraham's lead, holding back nothing, in faith that God would provide. I'd offered my own first fruits at the harvest festival, proud to demonstrate my devotion to the Law. I never thought Abraham's example was supposed to be a literal one, that I might one day be asked to give God my child. But God intervened for Abraham, miraculously providing a ram to take Isaac's place on the altar. Wouldn't he do the same for me? Couldn't the fever pass over her, like the plague passing over the Israelite firstborn in Egypt?

In the stuffy dimness of the room where my daughter lay dying, I pleaded with God, calling to mind the tales of Elijah and Elisha bringing children back to life – but for every story of miraculous recovery there was another, darker one: David, weeping for his son Absalom; Jephtha, who sacrificed his own daughter in fulfilment of a sacred vow. Faced with those stories, I found I had no appetite for being a hero of faith, or even a man of reputation and reliability. I would have traded all those things for my daughter. *Take away my wealth,* I said to God, *and give someone else charge of the synagogue. Just let her live.*

In desperation, I remembered the Nazarene who was hanging around the town. We weren't supposed to have anything to do with him – he was *persona non grata* in the synagogue after breaking the Sabbath laws – but to my shame I didn't care. Didn't they say he'd brought someone's son back from the dead down in Nain? Maybe he could save my daughter. Leaving my wife to watch the child, I slipped out. I found him down by the lake shore, trying to make himself heard above the crowd. When they saw I wanted to get to him, people stood back to let me through. (As I said, status has its advantages.) I'd imagined I would stand before him, man to man, and calmly ask for his help, but instead I found myself on my knees at his feet, wailing, "Help my daughter!" I could see people staring at me in astonishment, but to be fair to the Nazarene, he didn't hesitate. Perhaps he didn't know I was one of the people who'd had him barred from the synagogue. He came as quickly as he could, but even so there was an unbearable delay when some woman grabbed at him and demanded his attention for a few precious minutes. I think I feared then we were too late.

As we approached my house, I heard the wailing of mourners and knew for sure. Someone came bustling out and said the Nazarene's services were no longer needed. But he wasn't put off. He said something strange: "Don't be afraid." And politely but firmly he made his way into the house, up to the room where she lay, so peacefully you'd almost believe she was asleep. That's what the Nazarene said, and for a moment my heart leapt with impossible hope – but my wife shook her head. After losing three children, she knows what death looks like. The layers-out protested too. They're professionals; they wouldn't be preparing a body for burial if there was any doubt. But the Nazarene took no notice of any of them. As if she were quite well, he took my daughter's hand and gently told her to get up. It sounds absurd as I describe it now, but it seemed to me watching that a surge of life pulsed through his hand into her still body, as if he were charged with a hidden power that had no choice but to overflow at a touch.

All I can say for sure is that one minute she was certified dead, and the next she was sitting up in her bed. She looked a bit dazed, blinking slowly as if her eyes wouldn't focus. I found my heart beating so hard I could hardly breathe. Suddenly the room was full of activity. The mourners and layers-out were shooed away, and my wife hurried to find something for the girl to eat. But I just drank in the sight of my child – alive. The Nazarene was in a hurry to leave, but not before he'd made us promise not to tell anyone. I didn't understand that; you'd have thought he'd want the world to know what he'd done. My daughter was dead and he'd brought her back to life – a miracle as good as anything from the tales of Elijah.

Our family is restored, but as the euphoria fades I know that something has changed. I see now that I'm not a true son of Abraham; I wasn't ready to let my child go when God asked. I abandoned my principles to chase after a discredited faith-healer. When it came to it, the hope of holding on to my daughter was more important than the certainty of keeping the synagogue rules, rules I've built my reputation on. And yet, God did spare her, just as he spared Abraham's son. Only this time he didn't provide a sacrifice in her place – he just gave her back to us.

I've arranged for a generous thank offering, of course: an unblemished bull calf from my best herd. But it's only now that I begin to realise that the true price of my daughter's life might be something else: my social status. Word has gone round that the Nazarene came to my house, right into our private quarters. People have started to look at me oddly, especially the Pharisees, who are quick to sniff out any hint of impropriety. I wonder how long it will be before they relieve me of my role in the synagogue. I wonder what that will mean for my place in society, my influence over local decisions, my financial position. The security I have painstakingly built for my family feels suddenly precarious. My impetuous action has put our livelihood at risk. But how could I have done otherwise? The agonising minutes watching my daughter slipping away showed me that my social position was not the safety net I thought it was. With all my status, I was powerless to save her, and in those moments, saving her was all that mattered. If my reputation couldn't protect the miracle of her life, perhaps it's not worth very much after all. Did the healer have a point, when he took us to task in the synagogue for having the wrong priorities? When other people's approval becomes an end in itself, does it shut our eyes to what's really important?

I was so busy looking after my reputation, I took my precious daughter's life for granted, until it was almost too late. It took a crisis to break open my shell of self-sufficiency, and then suddenly God's mercy came flowing in like a river. So this is what I hope I can teach her one day: sometimes the certainty that we're doing the right thing is our greatest danger. And it turns out you can't make a true sacrifice out of duty – only love.

7

Cementing Power

The Death of John the Baptist

by Herod's jailer

MARK 6:14-19

I know what you're thinking: *Who cares what the jailer thinks?* But you'd be surprised at some of the stories I could tell. One thing about a job in the shadows is that you get to watch the big characters up close, and work out what makes them tick. Take Herod, for instance; it's quite an education to have a front-row view of his single-minded pursuit of power. How does one man control an entire province? If you're Roman, it's easy: soldiers and brute force. But Herod, client king that he is, has to use his wits. It's not for nothing they call him The Fox. His methods might be crude, but you have to admire his political deftness. Steering a course to keep Rome happy while keeping a lid on rebellion means always thinking two steps ahead.

He's suspicious of everything and everyone. So it was no surprise that the man they call the Baptiser ended up in jail. When the rumours first started, he sounded like a harmless nobody, boring on about repentance and recycling some old prophecies. But as his following grew, you could see Herod getting tense. He doesn't like large gatherings, unless he's organised them himself, and he's always alert to where the next uprising is brewing. Then the Baptiser sealed his fate by criticising Herod's personal life. That was never going to end well. Obviously we all know you shouldn't ditch your own wife to run off with your brother's. There are laws about those things. But if you're the king you get to decide which laws apply to you. If Herod says it's fine then it is fine – for him, anyway. So that was the end of the road for the Baptiser – arrested, roughed up, and chained to a dungeon floor, with no prospect of a trial and no time off for good behaviour.

When he arrived he looked as if he'd already been under lock and key for months: filthy, thin as a spear-shaft, eyes glittering with – what? – inspiration, or madness? He wasn't ranting; if anything he was quieter than I'd expected. But he did have an uncanny, almost mesmerising power. It wasn't long before the guards were stopping by the cell to ask his advice: "How should we live if we want to see God's salvation?" They know it's Herod who pays their wages and keeps order, but they're still superstitious enough to want some divine backup.

The Baptiser's answers were simple: "You know what you've done wrong; say sorry and start again. Practise charity and compassion – and do it now, because a new age is dawning and a new king is among us."

"Is it you?" they asked, half joking, half in awe.

He just laughed. "I'm not even worthy to serve as his slave! The king of heaven and earth is coming to claim his throne."

It was a wild statement from a wild man, but Herod was never going to let that threat pass once he'd got wind of it. He had the Baptiser summoned to his palace for questioning. Who is this new so-called king and what kind of power does he have? That would have been a good moment for the prisoner to change his story. It might even have saved his life, but the Baptiser wasn't one for backing down. For all his success at working a crowd, he really had no political sense whatsoever.

I watched from the door, ready to jump in at the first sign of trouble. It was almost funny to see the two of them squaring up to one another: the king in his robes and the prisoner in his filth. The Baptiser's influence was long gone, his followers scattered and his audience reduced to a few awestruck guards. Herod had already won this contest. He held all the authority – but the Baptiser didn't care. It was clear by then he wasn't raving; he just had no interest in saving his own skin. I've never seen anyone so relaxed facing the man who held the power of life and death over him. It gave him a kind of freedom which intrigued Herod. That evening, and those that followed, he questioned the Baptiser about his teaching, his intentions and his followers, but never managed to pin down any useful information. The prisoner had a way of speaking that made it hard to tell what was ancient prophecy and what he thought was real. He insisted he'd seen a man filled with the Spirit of the Almighty; he talked of a king ruling with a mighty arm, and in the next breath of a shepherd picking up injured lambs; he predicted a reign of justice and peace, where the strong give place to the weak and beggars bask in the favour of God.

That wasn't exactly a message to appeal to the king, but his conviction was so compelling that even hard-bitten Herod fell under his spell. It was as if he'd started to see the Baptiser as a sort of in-house holy man, like the voice of his silenced conscience. Otherwise he'd surely have had him struck down on the spot. The prisoner kept going on about Herod's new wife, how the marriage offended God's Law, and Herod must repent, just the same as the humblest of his subjects. He quoted the prophets – "the sanctuaries of Israel will be ruined; with my sword I will rise against the house of Jeroboam" – as if he expected the Assyrian army to ride into the palace that very moment. He didn't seem to realise that things are different now. The Romans are the new power-brokers and Herod needs all his wiliness to keep on the right side of them. Morals come a distant second behind political calculations. If anyone's going to be struck down by the sword, who is it likely to be: the king with his bodyguard and his alliances, or the prisoner making wild accusations?

And so it turned out. You've heard the story, about the girl dancing and the drunken promise made in front of hundreds of witnesses that couldn't be taken back. I think it's true: Herod *was* sad to see the end of the Baptiser; I think, for all his crazy talk, he was the only person who spoke to Herod like an equal, without fear. Herod has played a difficult game very skilfully, but he's always lived in fear: of the Romans, of rebellious subjects, of his own family. And not without reason. Already there are rumours that the father of his first, abandoned wife is raising an army of invasion on the border. People say that's the mark of God's anger – or even a curse called down by the Baptiser. But if you ask me, it's just part of the price of being a king. Once you reach the top, you might be surrounded by prestige and luxury, but you never stop looking over your shoulder for the next person who's trying to topple you.

In their unequal encounter, the prisoner had one huge advantage over the king: he had nothing to left to lose. At the height of his popularity he'd had power enough to give Herod sleepless nights, but he let it all go without a second thought. He went from being a man of influence, with hundreds of followers, to a nobody in a provincial jail, and it just didn't seem to bother him. He met his death without fear – with even a fierce kind of joy. Perhaps he knew all along that this was how it would have to end. His message mattered more to him than his own survival, as if his power came not from him, but from devotion to a cause that was stronger than death itself. Herod's one objective is holding on to power. The Baptiser only wanted to hand it over, and that made him invincible.

Now they're saying he's come back again, but I can tell you that's not true. I oversaw the execution. Trust me, there was no room for doubt. More important, I heard what he said: "I must die so that the glory can be his." Whoever he was talking about, that man has a power that Herod can only dream of.

8

A Day to Remember

Feeding the Five Thousand

by a mother

JOHN 6:1-13

I don't know what he thought we were going to see. My husband woke me early this morning in a buzz of excitement. "Get up, the healer's in town – you know, the miracle worker, that Nazarene that everyone's talking about. If we leave now we can get there early and have a good view."

When I'd roused myself enough to understand what he was on about, I asked him where we were going. He didn't know. What about the boy? "Bring him too!" He's not a practical man, my husband – always the big picture, never the detail. So we were setting off on a wild goose chase to find a miracle man somewhere in our region, who might decide to vanish the moment we got there, for all he knew. What about food and shelter? What if we ended up too far from home with nowhere to stay? How was the boy going to cope with all that walking? He's only six – little legs, but too heavy to carry these days. And I wouldn't think of leaving him; he's my only one now, since the fever took the babies. But when my husband gets an idea in his head it's hard to shift it – and if I'm honest I had a bit of a hankering to see the healer myself. So I sighed, and rolled out of bed, and set to putting together some provisions for the day: water, food, a cloak for when it gets cold later, a staff for balance or even as a makeshift weapon if we might need it.

Well, do you know, in the end he was right. It was the most wonderful day. We found the healer easily enough (so many people were doing the same as us, you didn't have to ask the way, just follow the crowd). And he was incredible. The miracles he did – you'd swear there was magic in his touch. But better than the miracles was the stuff he said – telling us a new era was dawning, when God's favour would return to our land and we would all be healed, the sad and the hungry, the persecuted and the bereaved. I thought of my little ones then. I don't often let myself do that; it doesn't do to be sentimental and the priests say we have to accept God's will. But when he spoke I let myself picture them, safe and happy somewhere they'd never be hungry or sad or ashamed, and it felt like a weight lifted from my shoulders. He had that gift of carrying you with him to a place you'd never imagined before. I could have listened to him all day.

As it turns out, we did. We watched and listened, never a murmur of complaint from the boy, who looked even more entranced than I was. When the shadows started to lengthen, the preacher fell silent. He looked worn out. He said he was going to pray, and set off up the mountain. And we all came too. What were we thinking? Thousands of ragged onlookers, scrambling after a man who'd just told us he wanted to be on his own. But we were hungry to hear more, to hold on to this vision of plenty he had laid out before us. I don't suppose many of that crowd were used to hearing good news. Like us, they'd struggle along with their heads down, aiming at survival and grateful for every day they have food on the table. We're insignificant in the grand scheme of things. Why wouldn't we follow a man who spoke to us as if we mattered?

Finally he stopped, and we all stopped too – and at that moment I think it suddenly dawned on us what we'd done. We were miles from home, night was falling and we'd eaten nothing all day. A murmur spread through the crowd. "Give us some food, prophet," shouted someone.

His supporters looked anxious, as well they might. There weren't nearly enough of them to fend off all these people. Was this where it would all get ugly? Then he said something to them, sending them into the crowd. Were they giving out money for bread? But where would we buy bread at night on a mountain? Thank goodness I'd had a bit of forethought; but it was going to be hard to eat our food without anyone else seeing.

One of the supporters, a Galilean, came our way. "Does anyone have any food to share?" he asked. Shaken heads, eyes turned down. No one was going to admit to it if they did.

And then the boy pipes up... "We have five loaves, and two fish: you can have those!"

I did have a moment of pride – he's so generous, my son, so positive and trusting. But he's like his father; he doesn't think. Where would our little picnic go among so many? And now we would be hungry, and so would they. Too late to protest – the Galilean was already going through the basket.

"Sardines!" he said. "Haven't tasted them in a while!" And he was gone – and with him, our dinner.

Well, after all, perhaps we owed the preacher a meal. He had entertained us all day. I hoped he'd get the fish; he looked as if he could use some feeding up. I'd have left then, but for some reason everyone started sitting on the ground. Was there going to be some final message?

The preacher began to pray, raising up his hands to the skies, but I couldn't hear his words. And then the followers started passing through the crowd again, and this time they really were doling something out. Had someone else had food to share? But surely there would have been nowhere near enough. And I didn't see any other families offering their bread. The same man, the Galilean, came towards us. "Have a sardine, little man," he said to my son. "You'll find it's a good one!" And he winked, and was off, handing out food as he went.

It was strange. The food we ate was so like what I had packed up this morning that I'd have sworn it came from my basket – except it was fresh and delicious, as if it were just out of the oven, and so filling I couldn't finish it. *This is what it must be like to live in a palace,* I thought, *and never feel hungry again.* Normally I'd have picked up the leftovers and hidden them in my cloak – there's always the next meal to worry about – but I was still under the spell of that wonderful food and the vision he'd given us, of a God spilling over in generosity to all his creation. So when the Galilean came back and asked if we had anything we'd like to give to the poor, it seemed the most obvious thing in the world to hand it over. Half a fish and most of a loaf. Now, looking back, I can't believe what I did. What are we, if not poor? But what a great feeling it was, to have enough to be generous for once in our lives!

It was a long, long journey home. The boy fell asleep and my husband had to carry him, which made us even slower. But we were so happy that night – as if our cares had been lifted off our shoulders, and we'd found space to breathe. We hadn't gone looking for healing, but it felt as if we were healed anyway, of that crippling weight of worry and anxiety: *What will we eat? When will the rains come? Will my boy grow up to be a man?* If he does, he'll remember this day. The glory of it was in his face all evening. "It was *our* fish, Mum; did you see? He made a miracle out of our dinner!"

I was still puzzling over the numbers. "How many do you think were there?" I asked my husband as we trudged home.

"Oh, five thousand, at least, I reckon," he said, "not counting the women and children."

I wasn't going to argue with him, but that made me smile. If you don't count the women and the children, who would have thought to bring the food to share? And who would have had the bright-eyed innocence to offer it?

9

Crossing Boundaries

Jesus in Tyre and Sidon
by the Canaanite woman

MATTHEW 15:21-28

The Jews hate us. That's no secret. We don't like them much, either. In the beginning it was all about land, but over the centuries a territory dispute has hardened into a statement of identity. Now they don't just look down on our culture and ridicule our beliefs. They loathe us from their guts. I know, because I've seen it for myself.

A few months back, my daughter fell ill with a disease no one could treat. It began with strange, random twitches in her limbs. Sometimes she would cry out as if she were in pain, although nothing had touched her. Or I'd find her gazing into space, unreachable, and afterwards she couldn't tell me where she had been. For days and even weeks at a time she would seem completely normal, and then out of nowhere the tremors would grip her again. When one day I saw her fall to the floor, writhing and jerking, I knew this was no ordinary sickness. People started to whisper she was demon-possessed and kept out of our way. I tried every doctor, every wise woman, but no one could help her. I was ready to despair by the time I heard of the Jewish miracle-worker travelling through the region around Tyre, and made up my mind to go and ask for his help. It was a long way to go for a faint hope, but what choice did I have?

As soon as I'd left the village, I started having second thoughts. People looked at me strangely, a woman travelling alone, and there were more than a few ribald comments I pretended to ignore. Then, as I approached the town, I was overtaken by a company of Jews. I could tell from their accents they weren't local, and they had that bravado of men outside their comfort zone, laughing a bit too loud, occasionally glancing over

Seeing the Light

their shoulders to see if anyone had overheard. They weren't concerned with me, of course; I was clearly no threat to anyone. Still, I pulled my hood over my face in the hope that I wouldn't be noticed and kept to the edge of the road. But as they were passing, one of them barged into me and suddenly I found myself at the centre of a small, menacing crowd.

"Canaanite scum!" said one man, and spat at my feet.

A man with a prayer shawl started muttering verses from the Bible: "I will drive out the Canaanites before you. Then you must destroy them totally. Make no treaty with them and show them no mercy."

One large man stepped in front of me, blocking my path, and said, "When the Messiah comes, he will drive all your people into the sea. Shall we start doing his work for him?"

Their bullying infuriated me. I almost answered back (which would have been a disaster), but at that moment a group of Phoenician traders came round the corner. The Jews hesitated, losing their appetite for a fight now they were outnumbered. There was a bit of arguing about who would pass first, and in the confusion I slipped away, taking a side road into the town.

After that, I was even more apprehensive about meeting the Jewish healer. I had a fair idea of the kind of reception I'd get, but having come this far I wasn't going to give up now. Finding him was harder than I thought, though. I'd imagined he would be somewhere public, doing his miracle show, but it turned out he wasn't holding court in the town square. Finally someone directed me to a dusty piece of scrubland just on the edge of the houses, where a group of Jews sat in the shade of a thorn tree. Seeing them, my heart tightened, but I noticed that there were some women there too, which gave me courage. Perhaps they'd be less likely to beat me up in front of their womenfolk.

I couldn't see anyone who looked like a miracle-worker, but he had to be one of them. I knew my best chance of being heard was to be polite, so I bowed low and said respectfully, "Master – have pity and heal my daughter!" No answer. I said it again, louder, and this time there was a murmur from the group. Keeping my head bowed, I called out a third time, addressing him by the name I'd been told he used: "Son of David, my daughter has a demon. Please heal her!"

One of the men got up and came over to me. "Woman, go away," he said. "The Master is resting. He hasn't come for people like you."

Something clenched in my gut when he said that. *What does he know of people like me? And what makes him think that he and his kind are so special that they can look down on us? My daughter is as precious as any Jewish child. Who is he to say that her sickness matters less than theirs?* I wasn't going to be deflected from my purpose by a self-important servant. It wasn't even him I was talking to. "Master, Son of David, have pity!" I said again, as loud as I dared.

The man who'd spoken turned his back on me but I kept on calling out. If you want to be heard in this world, you have to speak up. Finally, there was a movement among the group under the tree, and a figure I hadn't noticed before stood up. He wasn't tall or well-dressed or particularly noteworthy, but they treated him with such deference it was obvious he was the one I'd come to see. He came towards me, flanked by a couple of supporters. His face surprised me; he wasn't the showman I'd been imagining. He looked kind, but exhausted.

"I was sent only to gather the lost sheep of Israel," he said.

That confused me. *Who's gathering sheep? I thought he was a healer.* But I had to grab my chance. I dropped to my knees in the dust and asked once again for his help.

"It's not right to take away bread from the children and give it to the dogs," he said.

Oh, the arrogance of it – those Jews with their favoured-nation status! He wasn't going to help me because he thought I was beneath him. I could have cursed him then, but I thought of my daughter and her desperate need. If I could just hold on to my temper, maybe there was still a chance to talk him round. Let him humiliate me, if only he would heal her.

"True, Lord," I answered, "but don't forget that even the dogs are allowed to eat the scraps that drop from the table."

The other men tensed at that; I guess they don't like people answering back. But he bent towards me. "Woman," he said, as if he were paying proper attention for the first time.

I raised my head and looked straight at him. His face had changed; there was a new energy in his manner, and a look of understanding in his eyes which belied his harsh words.

"You have great faith. Your request is granted. Your daughter will be healed."

Before I could reply, the henchmen bustled him away and told me to be off. I didn't need telling twice. I wasn't keen to hang around a bunch of Jews, and it was obvious the miracle-worker had done all he was going to do. He said she would be healed. Did I believe him? I didn't know what to think, but as I trudged the long miles home, keeping to the small roads and tagging on to groups of other travellers where I could, I felt a strange hope rising in my heart.

When I reached my house, there was my daughter waiting for me, calm and in her right mind. I saw a lightness in her body that I hadn't even realised she'd lost, as if a weight had been lifted from her shoulders. Of course, it was many weeks before I could truly let myself believe she was cured – and even longer before the neighbours stopped crossing the road to avoid her. But something changed in her from the day of my foolhardy trip.

How did it happen? I've asked myself over and over again. How could a man drive out a demon from half a day's walk away? There was no incantation, no ritual, no berries or herbs to feed her. The only way I can explain it is to say that when he looked at me and I looked at him, something passed between us, as if by daring to question his words I had unlocked some secret door and he saw me not as an enemy but as a fellow child of God. Something about my stubbornness fired him up, exhausted and reluctant as he was, and connected him with a power that was outside of him. It reminded me of when lightning finds a tall tree and comes crashing down from the sky. He directed the miracle, but it didn't come from him. He drew on a force beyond himself, and it took shape in the space between us, born from my determination to save my daughter, and his unexpected compassion. He commended my *faith*, but that's not how I saw it. What drove me to kneel in the dust before a Jew, meeting his arguments on his terms and compelling him to hear me, was something fiercer and sharper than faith. I'd call it *love*.

10

Parting of the Ways

Jesus, the Bread of Life

by a disciple

JOHN 6:25-69

If you want to know why I left everything to follow the teacher, that's easy: he makes me feel alive like never before. I'm not talking about the miracles, although they are amazing. I don't even mean the excitement of being part of a movement, that sense of belonging to something bigger than myself, with my own unique role to play. It's more that he has a zest and a power about him, like a light burning inside that never goes out, and when you're with him everything feels bigger and brighter and more real. The best thing is when he sits everyone down and talks, and you can feel all the pieces falling into place. He explains the past and excites you about the future and makes you feel as if you're part of God's plan to transform the world.

I've heard plenty of speechmakers before – people using honeyed words to sway their audiences one way or another – but he's different. When their words fade away, you're left with a sense of emptiness, because clever rhetoric was all they had. With him, the words are powerful enough, but even so they won't stretch to contain his meaning, so there are always more questions to be asked, a feeling of a bigger truth just out of reach. Sometimes I think my brain just can't hold it all. But he's patient; he doesn't mind explaining over and over again, even though he must be as frustrated as we are at our slowness to understand.

Often he'll start with a simple story to put a picture in people's minds. Mostly the crowds are content with that. If they hang around, it's in the hope of a spectacle, something to gasp at and then retell around the fire on cold evenings. They don't really want the message spelled out, in case it might challenge them to change their thinking. But afterwards, when it's just us, he's usually happy to go further. If some of his explanations raise more questions than they answer, we've learnt to be patient. It will all become clear eventually. And when he talks, I feel myself overflowing with a sense of vitality and purpose – God's promise of hope and renewal, which we are going to help bring about.

Until today, that is. It all started with bread. He loves to use ordinary, everyday examples to create pictures of God's kingdom that everyone can imagine. This time, though, it was harder than ever to get people to focus on the kingdom. Everyone's heard about the miracle by the lake, where thousands of people were fed with just a few loaves. Not surprisingly, they were hoping for a repeat performance. But he's not interested in putting on a show for its own sake. You could tell he thought it was time to teach them to look beyond their everyday needs. So he said they should set their sights on eternal food, by following his teaching. People kept clamouring for a sign, and then someone remembered Moses giving our ancestors bread in the wilderness. They're still more interested in filling their bellies than in grappling with spiritual truths – and to be honest I don't really blame them. It's hard to care about the finer points of religion when you don't know where the next meal's coming from. But as he keeps reminding us, physical needs aren't everything, and his words link us to God and provide sustenance for the soul. And so he told them that he was the true bread from God, sent down from heaven to give life to the world. Not like Moses' manna in the desert, that barely lasted the day and was rotten by the next morning; not like our ordinary bread that hardens and moulds if it's kept too long. He has come to feed our souls with words of truth that will never fade.

There were some synagogue leaders in the crowd who didn't like that at all. They muttered about blasphemy, and someone pointed out that they knew exactly where he'd come from and it wasn't heaven; it was a carpenter's workshop in Nazareth. They summoned him to come and explain himself in the synagogue.

I wasn't prepared for what happened next. It made me realise that what we've seen up till now has been the simple bit. Even if the details are obscure, the core of his message has always had a compelling clarity. He spoke of the need for renewal and self-sacrifice. He punctured the self-importance of the Pharisees without ever deviating from the Scriptures. He channelled God's power into healing and restoring the lost. And when he made parallels with everyday life, it was always clear that he was talking in parables. But today in the synagogue, even I could see that he'd taken a new direction. First of all he coolly announced that all those whose hearts were truly committed to God would follow him. Then he repeated his claim, that he is the living bread from heaven, and that those who feed on him will find eternal life. The synagogue leaders took him literally; they scoffed at the idea that he could give them his own body to eat. That would have been the moment for him to explain that he wasn't talking about physical truths, but spiritual ones. But he didn't. He said it again, with added emphasis: only those who eat his body and drink his blood will have eternal life.

You can imagine how well that went down. He seemed to be promoting cannibalism. However lax you might be about dietary laws, every one of us would have our stomachs turned by that idea. And drinking human blood, when we've been taught from the cradle that even animal blood is forbidden, sacred to God and reserved for the altar? It sounded like the disgusting stories of heathen warriors drinking the blood of their defeated adversaries. How could we picture ourselves drinking his? He'd suddenly changed from a harmless miracle-worker to a weird occultist, and maybe a blasphemer too. The crowd grew hostile. The synagogue officials were looming ominously. It was time to get him out of there before he caused a riot. Thankfully, the authorities were content to let him go. Perhaps they were worried about upsetting his followers – although I don't think he's made himself many friends in this town. I find it hard to grasp what I heard myself, and I'm used to musing over his oblique sayings.

No one dared comment at the time, but later when we sat to share bread, and he blessed it and broke it and handed it out, I had a sudden nauseating vision of us tearing at his lifeless flesh and stuffing it into our mouths. From the looks on others' faces, I wasn't alone.

"Master," I began, "this talk of eating your body and drinking your blood... It's a hard teaching; how are we to understand it?"

"Are you offended by my words?" he asked. "Do you need to see me ascend into heaven before you can believe? I came from the Father and I will return to the Father, and everything I tell you is full of his Spirit. The Spirit gives life, and the flesh is useless. But only the Father chooses who can hear."

I was still none the wiser. He often talks about the life of the Spirit, about how we must worship God with our hearts and minds, and not get stuck on ritual obedience. I have cheerfully abandoned my livelihood to travel with him, because I believe God's truth is in his words, and God's

Spirit flows through him. I know he comes from God, and I know that his words have the message of life. But this talk of eating his actual body frightens me. It's as if he wants to turn mystical truth into a physical reality, to tie the spiritual realm into the material world. We all know how important symbols are, like the bread we share at the table representing fellowship and unity and God's provision for us. But his words in the synagogue took an altogether darker turn. He is our leader. I believe he will be our king. How can he also be our food? Is he saying that to find eternal life we have to kill him? But then how is he going to lead us to the kingdom of God?

I wasn't the only one to feel confused. It was noticeable that people started to make excuses to leave after that, even one or two of the inner circle. He made no complaints; it was as if he'd expected exactly this. Perhaps it was a test of our commitment.

"Do you want to leave too?" he asked those of us who were left.

There was an uncomfortable silence. Then Peter (swift to speak, slow to think, as always) jumped in to fill it. "Where else would we go? You have the words of eternal life."

For once, Peter wasn't wrong. He *does* have the words of life, words that heal and restore and bring hope where there was none. That's why we follow him, even when things are hard.

But I've started to think that the words he speaks are not just pictures, but doors. They remind me of the gates of the great temple in Jerusalem, so beautiful and richly carved that you could just stand and admire them for their artistry, but their true purpose is to be a gateway to another world. Beyond them is something majestic and glorious, and at the same time mysterious and foreboding. All this time we've been looking at the shining surface of his words, and now he's nudged the door open and shown us what lies behind: a mystery too big for any of us to grasp, where life and death, body and spirit are all gathered up into the great incomprehensible truth at the heart of God. I won't give up on him now. I've thrown in my lot with him, and I trust that his words hold the secret of life. But now he's hinting there will be death there too, and how those two things can be woven together into victory is a question that only God can answer.

11

Peter Climbs a Mountain

The Transfiguration
by Peter

MARK 9:2-9

I'll be honest: I don't much like mountains. All that climbing, the sun beating down on your back and your legs screaming for mercy – and what do you find when you get to the top? Rocks and wind, mostly. I know there are views, but I'd rather be on level ground looking up at a mountain than on the top of one looking down.

But the teacher has always had a thing about high ground. It gets him away from the crowds, gives him space to think. More often than not he heads off by himself, which always makes me uneasy. Who will look out for him while he's lost in his prayers? So this time, when he asked three of us to come with him, it was a relief. He's been in a strange mood lately, talking about plots and violence and catastrophe. I don't see how that fits with his message of peace and plenty. If he's God's chosen Messiah (and he pretty much admitted it, even though we're not supposed to say anything), shouldn't he be leading a triumphal army? But I should know by now that he never comes at things the way you'd expect. When I tried to talk him down from his gloomy predictions, he turned on me – called me Satan, if you can believe it! That really stung. I make my share of mistakes, for sure, but since the moment he turned up by the lake in Galilee I've given up everything for him: my job, my family, my home. And he knows I'd do anything to keep him safe. So I suppose being invited on one of his mountain walks felt like a kind of olive branch.

It was as bad as I'd expected: an exhausting climb through that thorny scrub that rips at your legs, with no hint of a breeze. The air started to feel thinner than normal, as if we'd reached a place made for birds, not humans. Is this what he means by being close to heaven? If it is, I'm not sure it's for me. Give me flat land, civilization and a practical problem to solve, and then I can be useful. But the truth is he only half belongs in that world. You could see it as he climbed, how the weariness dropped off him. While we stumbled behind, he surged on like an eagle riding an air current. And when we finally stopped, his whole face had changed. It was as if he were drawing the sun itself into his body, until he glowed with a light from within. Even his clothes were dazzling, white as a fresh fall of snow.

When I could stop squinting, I had the shock of my life. There were two men talking to him. Where did they spring from, on that bare mountain? Was he in danger? But they carried no obvious weapons and it all looked friendly enough. Very slowly it dawned on me: these weren't ordinary people. They were dressed in the robes of desert nomads from long ago, and shining with that same unearthly light. Out of nowhere, two names came into my head: Moses, and Elijah. It was like the moment when the teacher asked us who we thought he was, and I found my lips saying "Messiah". Look, no one would call me the brains of our group. I'm not a strategist like Judas. I don't have John's gift for poetic language, or Mary's imagination. I certainly don't hear voices or see visions. But sometimes I just know things, and this is what I knew then. Moses, the law-giver, and Elijah, the great prophet, stood there on the mountain, speaking with our teacher. Had they summoned him, or had he summoned them? Or were we perhaps not in our world any more? Had we climbed right through the sky into heaven? Moses, Elijah and the Messiah – the Law, the Prophets and the King-to-be. The three of them were like the completion of a circle, the fulfilment of the promise of long ago.

I don't mind saying that right then my knees were trembling so I could hardly stand. But at the same time I wanted to stay there for the rest of my life, out on the bare mountain where the world made sense. Nothing else mattered, not the petty quarrels between us, not our miserable failure to heal people, not even the way my words had offended him. This was God bringing everything together, and I wanted to be part of it. I knew I should keep my mouth shut but the words came out anyway: "Teacher, how lucky we're here! Let us build three dwellings for you." Even as I spoke, I could hear how ridiculous I sounded. Did I really think three fishermen could rig up shacks out of thorn scrub fit for Israel's mythical heroes?

Peter Climbs a Mountain

He didn't reply. I don't think he even heard me. *God* replied. I know, I've said already, I don't do visions. I don't have prophetic dreams or see angels. But I did hear this, as surely as I once heard the teacher saying, "Follow me." "This is my Son," said God, "the one I love; listen to him!" And as the voice spoke the light got brighter and brighter, until all the glory of heaven was showering down on him. When I could open my eyes again, the other two figures were gone. None of us dared to approach him, so we watched from a distance while he prayed. Then, with hardly a word, he led us back down the mountain, back to our ordinary lives.

Since then, though, I've noticed a difference in him. He always had a sense of purpose, but now it's redoubled. He talks about time running out, and his instructions come so fast no-one can keep up. But then, I don't feel quite the same, either. I wish I could recapture that feeling of everything making sense, seeing the bigger picture, not just what's in front of my face. The other evening, someone was telling the story of Elijah, whisked up into heaven in a chariot of fire. I used to think that was mostly a fairy tale, but now... I wonder. If God visits our world, wouldn't it be in just that kind of a blaze of glory? And I noticed a detail I hadn't heard before, about Elisha. He set off on that last journey as Elijah's loyal servant, but he came back changed. It wasn't long before he'd stepped right into his master's shoes: feeding the hungry, healing the sick, raising the dead. What if that's what seeing God's glory up close does to you? What if it opens the door to possibilities you never knew you had?

Elisha walked all the way to the Jordan, and we climbed a mountain to see it. But now I ask myself if the light and splendour and truth isn't always there, just on the edges of our sight, like a fish that doesn't quite break the surface of the water. If you're not paying attention it looks like a flash of sunlight, but follow its silvery glint and it can lead you to a shoal rich enough to overflow your nets. You just have to know what to look for. Up there on the mountain, you couldn't miss God's glory. Now that I've seen it, I find myself catching glimmers of it in all sorts of unexpected places: the kindness of strangers, the times we put aside our differences and make peace with each other, the small joy of sharing a meal at the end of a long day.

The memory of what happened that day is like a lamp shining in a dark place. When I doubt myself, or I doubt his message with its dismal undertones, I remember that dazzling light, and the feeling that everything fitted together. I remember hearing the voice of God. The teacher still says things which scare me, and some which make no sense at all. I have a feeling there will be more mountains to climb before the end. But God told us to listen to him, and that's what I'm going to do, wherever it takes me and whatever it costs.

12

Family Tensions

Jesus at the Home of Mary and Martha
by Martha

LUKE 10:38-42

I stood in the kitchen, where the fire smoked and sulked, grinding my teeth to stop myself screaming. Why is it always me left to deal with the practical arrangements? Why, in all the excitement of having the teacher in our house, does not one person think of the work that goes on behind the scenes? And where is my sister while I'm carrying the weight of the household?

I knew where she was, of course. Mary was in there with the men, like some queen basking in the approval of her court. She glanced over her shoulder at me as she slipped into the room, and in her face I could see her knowledge that she shouldn't be there, but also a sparkle of delight at her own daring. Mary has always got away with things. No one can help being charmed by her easy self-confidence. She wins your heart with a single smile, and hardly anyone can say no to her. She radiates joy, and people love her for it, and that makes her even happier. Even I can't help warming to her, and I know what her carelessness costs. I'm not like Mary. I learnt early that making myself useful was the way to win praise. "Martha's such a good little helper," my mother's friends would say. I liked being helpful. I liked being wanted. I learnt to be efficient, reliable, resourceful – and dull. Slowly, over the years, our roles solidified around our personalities. Lazarus was the boy, the leader, the host, growing up to be the head of the household. Mary was its vivacious heart. I was the hidden framework that held it all together, the bones and sinews doing the heavy lifting for the sake of the others. Most of the time, it worked well as an arrangement. It played to our strengths and allowed us each a role that we could fill to our satisfaction. But just sometimes, I felt the creeping tendrils of bitterness tightening their hold on my heart.

What riled me this time was that the teacher was only there because of me. I was the one who'd invited him into our house, and now I was exiled to the kitchen while the other two lapped up his stories. The last flame guttered and went out, and my patience snapped. I went to the curtain of the main room and lifted it.

"Mary," I hissed, "I need some help."

If she heard me, she gave no sign. She'd wormed her way to the front of the room, right at the feet of the teacher, and she sat gazing up at him, drinking in his words. Why had no one sent her away? Had it not occurred to Lazarus that she was bringing dishonour on the whole family? But the teacher is odd like that; there are plenty of stories about him tolerating scandalous breaches of social etiquette. If someone complains, he'll brush it away, as often as not. I don't mean that he doesn't care about doing the right thing, it's just that he seems to have fewer rules about what's right and what's not. So he's relaxed about children interrupting, or about being seen with people with a shameful reputation. I suppose that might even extend to a woman sitting in a roomful of men. But even the teacher needs to eat, not to mention the crowds who follow him around. And for that, I needed help in the kitchen.

Mary had her back to me and I didn't know how to get her attention. So far, no one else had noticed me. The only person facing in my direction was the teacher, and I counted on the shadows at the back of the room to keep me hidden. But I had reckoned without his extraordinary perception. He paused in his speaking and looked straight at me, and I felt suddenly weary of hiding my feelings behind a mask of politeness. If he has come to preach justice to the world, perhaps he could start in our house.

"Master, don't you care? My sister sits here doing nothing while I'm rushed off my feet. I need her to help me." As soon as I'd said it, I regretted my outburst. What was I thinking, exposing our family tensions in public like that?

"Martha," he began, gently, and I dropped my head in shame, waiting for the inevitable reprimand. Now he had seen the ugliness of my anger, who could blame him for favouring my sister? But he didn't scold me. He said my name again, "Martha," and waited, as if we were the only two people in the room and he needed me to give him all my attention.

When I met his eyes I didn't see condemnation, only a perceptive kindness. Something about the quality of his gaze made me feel seen as I had never been seen before. It was as if he were looking right through my superficial, busy usefulness into the confusion of feelings battling in my heart, and suddenly I could see them properly for the first time too: resentment, unfulfilled hopes, and behind them all a secret unspoken fear.

"You are worried," he said, "and you have so many things that make you anxious and upset."

It wasn't an accusation: his words were full of sympathy, as if he too knew what it was like to carry the weight of other people's needs. No one has ever quite grasped what it's like to live sandwiched between my happy-go-lucky brother and my adorable, unconventional sister. But he did, and in his understanding I felt my ragged emotions soothed and contained.

"There's only one thing you really need," he said. "Look! Mary has chosen it, and it won't be taken away from her."

I felt the bitterness rise in me again. That was all very well for him to say. Did he think the dinner would cook itself? Did he expect us to turn away a dozen hungry men and women from our house without refreshment, breaking all the laws of hospitality? He might talk about being sustained by the word of God, but even the teacher needs food and drink at the end of the day. I suppose I shouldn't have been surprised by his casual disregard for household work; after all, what does a man know of lighting fires, gutting fish, stretching supplies meant for a family to feed a crowd? But I did think he cared about justice. Mary has been choosing the easy path for years while I clear up behind her. Don't my needs count for anything?

I let the curtain fall again and went back to the kitchen. What did he mean, there is one thing I really need, and Mary has chosen it? Just then, what I needed was a helping hand, and she had certainly not chosen that. But a quiet voice in my head cut through my anger. What if what I craved most of all was actually that gentle understanding, the sense of finally being recognised and accepted for myself? Acceptance comes easily to Mary because everyone loves her. I've learnt to settle for earning gratitude for my service – but the truth is that people are rarely grateful for the things you do for them all the time. So you get caught in a cycle of trying harder for less reward, making yourself busier and busier, bewildered that the payoff never comes.

Face to face with the teacher, I'd had a momentary glimpse of what it might be like to feel secure, valued for myself, not for my service to the household. In his eyes I saw that I mattered, to him and to God, and that fleeting knowledge made me hungry for more. Is that what God has been saying to us all along? All the rules about ordered living – are they missing the point? "You shall love the Lord your God with all your heart," we're taught – but what if God loves us back the same way? What if God loves me – dull, dutiful Martha – not for my hard work but because he sees into my heart and values what he finds there? And at the same time he values Mary for her qualities and Lazarus for his, rejoicing in our uniqueness and holding us all together so that we can rejoice in each other too.

It felt like a door opening on a dark room, allowing me to see clearly for the first time. My fear and resentment, weaving around my sense of duty like a cage, were trapping me in the role of a put-upon drudge. But I could choose to set them aside. I could walk back through the curtain and sit at the teacher's feet, and let his voice heal the wounds in my soul. Still, something made me hesitate. This knowledge felt too new, and too intimate for such a public setting. I wanted to live with its strangeness for a while, adjusting to its unfamiliar shape in my mind. Absentmindedly I stoked the fire which had finally caught, recalling the warmth of the teacher's attention, his unspoken offer of love and welcome, even though I'd come to him full of bitterness and accusation.

All at once I wanted to do something special for him – to thank him for noticing me. What if I were to use my skills in the kitchen to create a feast for him? (He might speak in the tradition of the ascetics, but when it comes down to it he does love a feast.) I measured out the grain and began to grind it, the same monotonous task I've performed a thousand times, but for once my labour had a meaning which went beyond drudgery. To my surprise, I found myself singing under my breath.

I'm not naïve enough to think that everything will be changed by this moment. I will carry on being challenged by Mary's heedlessness and Lazarus's extravagance. We will still argue over who does what in the house. But I have made a silent promise to myself that I will not get trapped again into working harder and harder to earn respect. I will remind myself how it felt to be valued, to be invited to the place where my needs can be met. I will hold on to the knowledge that being recognised and loved is a gift God is just waiting to give.

13

The Price of Success

Jesus and the Rich Young Man

by a servant

MARK 10:17-31

Something is eating at my master. He hasn't stopped going about his business; if anything, he's more active than ever, overseeing building plans, checking stewards' reports, managing his handouts to the poor. But he looks haunted. Just last week, he asked out loud what more he needed to do to earn God's favour. He had me read to him from his favourite scriptures: proverbs about wealth and good living. "Wisdom says, 'I walk in the ways of righteousness, along the paths of justice, bestowing a rich inheritance on those who love me and making their treasuries full.'" My master seemed to be listening, but the next moment he waved me away and went back to his accounts, totting up what he'd earned, checking the profits on his ventures.

What is it that makes him so uneasy? I swear, he has so much money that he could lose three quarters of it in a barn fire and still live in luxury. That kind of wealth turns some men into petty tyrants, thinking they're answerable to no one, not even God. But my master is very devout. He's always been scrupulous about giving time to his prayers, and his tithes are calculated to the penny. And as anyone can tell, it's paid off. God has seen his righteousness and endowed him with wealth in return, just as the proverb says. If I were him, I'd take that as divine approval and count my blessings. But lately my master seems obsessed by the idea that his good fortune can't last. He mumbles other, darker proverbs, about people who build grand houses but don't survive to live in them. He asks himself if his success isn't built on the oppression of others. I think he's splitting hairs. Someone has to come out on top, and at least he tries to use his wealth wisely.

The Price of Success

But the rich get to do things their own way, and my master's way is always to ask questions – and then have me find out the answers for him. So it wasn't entirely unexpected when he said to me, "There's something missing. God has favoured me for now, but how can I be sure of the future? Find me someone who can tell me the secret of eternal life."

I would have laughed, if I'd dared. Eternal life? Not even the rabbis can agree over that. Some say there's nothing but a void after death; as God told Adam, "Dust you are, and to dust you will return." Some follow the teaching of the prophet Daniel: "Multitudes who sleep in the dust of the earth will awake, some to everlasting life, others to shame and everlasting contempt." But no one can tell you for a certainty which is true. Still, my master is not one to take no for an answer, so I bowed my way out, with a silent prayer that this particular obsession might be a fleeting one.

And then I remembered the teacher from Nazareth. Travelling preachers are two a penny round here – and rarely worth listening to. But by chance I had caught the end of a story this one told, about a rich man and a beggar in the afterlife. There was some moral (I don't remember what) but it was definitely about eternal life – paradise with Abraham, or torment in Hades. Personally I doubt if this teacher knows any more than the next man about eternity, but my master likes answers, the quicker the better. Here at least was one to offer him.

"I want to meet this man," he said – and what my master wants, he usually gets. We had to go to him, mind you, and there was no private audience, just a conversation in the open street with all the peasants gawping. Even so, my master treated him with reverence, kneeling before him in the dust, as if the teacher were the rich, successful one.

The teacher, for his part, seemed completely unimpressed by my master's retinue, his expensive clothes or his well-bred compliments. In fact, he was verging on rude. "You know the commandments," he said. Then he listed a few, as though he thought my master might have forgotten them.

"I have done all this," said my master, just a hint of frustration in his voice.

I thought the preacher would commend him for his piety. But instead he looked at my master kindly, almost as if he were bestowing a favour on him. "There's one thing you're missing. Sell your possessions and give the money to the poor. Your treasure will be kept for you in heaven. Then follow me."

Seeing the Light

I couldn't believe my ears. Sell all his possessions? Give away his hard-earned cash – the very symbol of God's approval? Traipse after a wandering prophet like some unemployed labourer hoping for a handout? My master *gives* the handouts! If he had no wealth, how could he show generosity to his neighbours? If he went on the road with this preacher, how would he fulfil his duty to his family? I half expected him to have the man whipped for impertinence, but instead he looked taken aback, even disappointed. Without another word he rose to his feet, bowed once and left. I hurried after him, but not before I heard the preacher say to the crowd, "How hard it is for the rich to enter God's kingdom – as hard as trying to thread a needle with a camel!" He was playing for laughs, of course, and he got them, but I was furious. How dare this upstart criticise my master? Did he think he had all the answers because he could entertain a crowd? What did he know of eternal life anyway? The truth is, none of us knows what heaven is like, certainly not this opinionated Nazarene.

But somehow or other his words have got under my master's skin. Now when he looks at his tally of wealth he sighs, as if he finds it a burden, not a security. When he talks about his responsibilities it's no longer as a source of pride, but a shackle. He takes no pleasure in fine clothes or sumptuous meals. The only thing that lifts his despondency is to have me read proverbs to him, and this is the one he keeps coming back to: "Wealth is worthless in the day of wrath, but righteousness delivers from death."

It makes no sense to me. Why is a young man suddenly obsessed with death? Why would someone blessed with riches and status give up on success in this life for a future which might not even exist? He's got all the benefits money can buy, and it still doesn't make him happy. That's not how things are supposed to be! I see at close quarters how his wealth weighs on him, how it cuts him off from other people even as it insulates him against disaster. He's become suspicious of everyone and everything. I suppose the teacher's words offered a vision of escape from all that obsessive financial planning. I did notice that – ragged as they were – his followers had a kind of freedom about them. They didn't know where they would be sleeping that night, or even where the next meal was coming from, but they had each other, and a sense of purpose and a leader they believed in, and an absolute trust that God would provide for them.

Even so, I can't help thinking that placing all your bets on the afterlife is a risky strategy. Which of us can control what happens when we die? In the end, all anyone can do is hope for God's mercy. An irresistible (and surely blasphemous) picture comes into my mind. There's a camel struggling to squeeze through an enormous needle, hump and belly stuck fast, legs flailing wildly – and God, giving it an almighty shove to set it free.

14

Who Rules Israel?

Paying Taxes to Caesar
by a Pharisee

MATTHEW 22:15-22

Jerusalem was heaving. It's always frantic at the lead-up to Passover, but this year seems busier than ever. Pilgrims, traders, temple officials, all jostling together in the narrow streets, not to mention the Roman soldiers, strutting around as if they own the place. Up on the Temple Mount the air was buzzing with a sense of expectation. It's hard to teach in front of so many curious visitors, while still keeping a sense of holiness for the festival.

You're surprised at that. I know everyone likes to put the Pharisees down; they call us killjoys and they think we're only interested in telling other people what to do. But let me just set the record straight for a moment. Our purpose is to call people back to true religion. Over the years it's got so watered down that if we're not careful our unique Jewish identity will be lost. The whole point of the Pharisaic revival is to get back to the purity of the old days. When we're a proper God-fearing society again, God's favour will return to us, and then we'll be able to throw off this foreign occupation and fulfil our destiny as his chosen people.

Well, I mustn't get carried away with dreams of the future. At least the Romans tolerate our religion. And that's one reason we have to tread such a fine line with them. We can't afford to antagonise them while they're in charge. Of course we want to see them gone – no self-respecting Jew doesn't – but all this agitating just plays into their hands. There's no chance of a rebellion taking off in any case. Say what you like about the Romans, they're ruthless enforcers. So we keep our eyes on religious law, and try to encourage the people to do the same. If only everyone would

Who Rules Israel?

follow God's commandments, things would be different. But they do need a bit of help. God's Law is a lamp for our feet and a light to our path, but it's also the testimony of his infinite, unknowable wisdom. Not everyone has the chance to meditate on its complexities – and that's where we come in. We help to clarify the details and point out where people might unknowingly be tripping up. We're providing a service really, if they could only see it.

Back to my story. Jerusalem was bursting at the seams. To make matters worse, one of those crackpot preachers had arrived from up north, with a whole sea of followers in tow. They turn up sometimes, claiming to be the Messiah, God's chosen instrument to bring about his new kingdom. They're all ridiculous, of course, but this one was more unbelievable than most. God's anointed king, surrounded by a ragtag army of lepers, prostitutes and children? Don't make me laugh. Oh, he had charisma all right, and you could see the people lapping up his stories. The Romans were keeping a close eye on him; any popular movement always raises the alert. I couldn't see this one taking off though – where were his soldiers? Even so, no one wants to upset the delicate balance of power, so we were watching closely too.

And of course, it wasn't long before he came after the religious establishment, taking swipes at the temple management and – can you believe it? – calling us hypocrites. Us, who comb the Scriptures for God's instructions and share them with the people! It was infuriating, but we had to tread carefully. His followers might be unarmed but there are plenty of them, and the last thing we want around Passover is a riot. To begin with we tried maintaining a lofty indifference, but he kept popping up in the temple courtyard, wanting to debate with us. Of course, he's misguided, but he's clever with it, and he certainly knows his Scripture. He's got an answer for anything.

Today, though, we really thought we had him nailed. The people think he's their next king. The Son of David, they call him – and who is the Messiah but David's son? (Of course, most of them have a very unsophisticated concept of the Messiah. He's nothing more than a freedom fighter as far as they're concerned – they have no idea of the judgement of the righteous, or the coming kingdom of God.) But the preacher isn't saying if he is or isn't the chosen one. He's playing his cards close to his chest, biding his time, so we came up with a way to get him to declare himself. We collected witnesses, and set him up with a simple question: Is it lawful to pay tax to the emperor? If he says no, that's the end of the road for him. The Romans will whisk him off and crucify him for insurrection. If he says yes, that's the end of the road for his movement. The prophecies say that the Messiah will reign over David's kingdom and shatter the yoke of the oppressor. You don't do that by meekly paying taxes to a foreign overlord, and the people know it. They'll lose faith and wander off to follow some other zealot. Either way, we can breathe easier again and Passover will be safeguarded for another year.

Except that's not quite what happened. He thought about the question for a moment. Then he asked for a Roman coin, held it up and asked what was on it. Any fool knows that – at least anyone who's had to pay the tax. The emperor, in all his glory, with his imperial titles and his pretensions to being a god. Even thinking of it makes my flesh crawl. There is no God but the Lord Almighty. Who is this Caesar with his pomp and status, who wants us all to bow down to him? I hoped the preacher would drop the coin in the dust. Instead, he handed it back. "Give to the emperor what belongs to the emperor," he said. "And give to God what belongs to God." That was all. Some of the people looked a bit disappointed. So, pay your taxes, then – not just the imperial tax but the temple tax as well. But to be honest I don't think that's all he meant. Hovering behind his words was another, more subtle message.

Let the emperor be, he seemed to be saying, with his delusions of grandeur and his imperial titles. Let him have his gold coins. It's all insignificant beside the glory of our God. I thought of the words of the prophet Isaiah, how even the heathen ruler Cyrus was an instrument of God. Isn't Caesar also under God's hand? All the power and wealth of the world is nothing in God's sight, for creation belongs to him alone. Just for a moment an image of a different kind of future swam into my head, of a ruler who doesn't rely on money and power and soldiers to cement his kingdom; where no one has to jostle for status and influence because everyone belongs. The words of another prophecy came back to me: "Here is my chosen servant in whom I delight ... he will not break a bruised reed or snuff out a smouldering wick." The rabbis say that's also a prediction of the Messiah. But it doesn't sound much like a conquering hero; no ruler I ever heard of won control of a kingdom that way.

It's left me with a strange, dislocated feeling, like when a curtain has been drawn aside, but your vision hasn't yet adjusted to the light. Whatever you make of this preacher, he challenges you to think. The second part of his answer sticks in my mind: Give to God what belongs to God. We know what the Law says: "Love the LORD your God with all your heart and with all your soul and with all your strength." Such a simple proposition, yet so hard to do, even with all our codes of behaviour to help us. At least we Pharisees are trying, not like the preacher and the messy rabble he surrounds himself with. But all the same, I can't help wondering: Has this 'Galilean nobody' chanced on a nugget of truth? Are all our careful political strategies actually getting in the way of our service to God?

The preacher's followers haven't abandoned him yet, although it's only a matter of time. They'll come to realise he won't lead them to glory. His kind only ever ends up on the gallows. But you have to hand it to him: he has the knack of making every one of them feel wanted, no matter what they are or what they've done. It reminds me of that psalm, "He will take pity on the weak and needy, for they are precious in his sight." Almost as if God's kingdom were already here.

15

Telling the Truth

Jesus on Trial
by Pilate

JOHN 18:28-19:16

No one messes with Rome. And no one messes with the Roman governor. I have a position of respect to maintain. As Rome's representative in Judaea, Samaria and Idumaea, I expect obedience, deference and submission. If you're tempted to disagree, I have several divisions of soldiers on hand to teach you the error of your ways, not to mention three legions stationed just over the Syrian border. I think you'll find I've been a pretty effective governor. Tax receipts are creditable, and Rome's coffers are the better by thousands of sesterces; the local kings (so-called) are all behaving themselves; we've even done some public works to keep the plebs happy. Now they have water piped right into Jerusalem. Are they grateful? Of course not.

    I don't want to give the impression it's all been plain sailing. Judaea's a tricky little number. All the petty local politics you find in every province, every year a whisper of rebellion somewhere – and I've never come across a people so touchy about religion. Once they've seen the Roman military in action, most places are grateful just to knuckle down and stay out of trouble. They get freedom to worship their gods as long as they recognise ours. Sounds a fair deal to me, but the Jews are a stubborn lot and they have an obsession with their God being the only show in town. It takes a strong hand and a cool head to maintain discipline without inciting revolt. Fortunately I am an excellent judge of character, and now I've got Caiaphas, their high priest, just where I want him. I give him the illusion of a bit of control, so he can take the responsibility for keeping the lid on any religious trouble. In return, he tells me what his spies are hearing from the rabble, so I can deal with any unrest before it gets out of hand. I will admit, things occasionally get a bit nasty. There was the time a new detachment of soldiers arrived to take up station in Jerusalem, with the imperial medallions on their standards. Just normal procedure, but the local priests made a huge fuss about the image of the divine emperor being brought into the city, and before I knew it there was a full-blown riot. The soldiers showed their worth that day. I had it all tidied up within the week – a few judicial executions to show who was in charge – but now the troops leave their standards outside the city. No point in creating trouble if you can avoid it.

Not that there isn't trouble always brewing in Judaea. The Jews just love to argue – they're as bad as the Greeks for that. In the courts, in the marketplace, in the temple itself. No wonder this country's forever being invaded; before they could get an army together they'd have to summon a council to debate recruitment and tactics. But they love a zealot, and every spring there's a new loudmouth, trailing a collection of misfits from some provincial town, promising freedom and prosperity and who knows what other nonsense. Most of them fizzle out of their own accord, but part of my job is to make sure none of the threats ever become serious. So when I got wind of this 'Son of Man' coming from out in Galilee, I paid attention. There had been rumours for a while, but nothing that smelled like danger. A few conjuring tricks and some irresponsible talk – just entertainment for the farmworkers really. My ears pricked up when I heard he'd arrived in Jerusalem just before Passover, though. There's always the risk of trouble at festivals, and I'd been planning to go there myself, just in case, even though at that season it's much pleasanter to stay in Caesarea. But I'm not here for my health; I'm a servant of Rome. So I made the trip to Jerusalem, and got Caiaphas to tell me what he knew. It goes without saying he wasn't too happy about the Galilean either. Caiaphas knows well enough that now he's hitched his chariot to the Romans, he'd be lynched as a collaborator without our protection. But there was something else about this preacher that really got under his skin. I didn't follow all the details (unlike the Jews, I don't go in for theoretical arguments) but he'd obviously breached some big religious taboo.

After that, it wasn't entirely unexpected when Caiaphas' men dragged him into the palace shouting about a trial, although I would have preferred it if they'd chosen a more convenient time. First light on the day before Passover? I had plenty to do without sorting out some internal religious squabble. It was clear he wasn't any kind of military threat. Caiaphas himself said his supporters had all evaporated the moment they brought him in. But sometimes it's useful to show the firm hand of Roman justice. And perhaps I was just a little bit intrigued. According to Caiaphas, he was claiming to be a king. Well, he clearly wasn't that. A madman, then? – but he didn't behave like someone deluded. On the other hand he wasn't trying to wriggle out of the accusation either, like any sane person would.

When I questioned him, he seemed to have no idea of the seriousness of his situation. Maybe he was a bit soft in the head. He wouldn't give me a straight answer, just went on about his kingdom, and how his servants were from another place. That made no sense. In this job, you get to know about how power works. If you want your kingdom to be recognised, you bring your servants and soldiers with you. Without slaves there is no Rome, and without the legions there would be no Empire. The preacher was clearly on a hiding to nothing, with his followers routed and his friends busy saving their own skins. But he wouldn't give up. Then he started on another tack: he was the truth-teller, whose destiny was to reveal the truth. I could tell he was trying to pull me into a debate, one of those endless religious arguments that go round and round in ever smaller circles, dwindling to an invisible point with no discernible purpose, unless you find satisfaction in pondering the eternal essence of the universe. But I'm a practical man and I have no time for cosmic niceties. What is truth? Truth is power. If you have the soldiers, you can make the world what you want it. If you're alone and friendless, you can have the best arguments ever but you're shouting in the wind. I'm here as the representative of Rome, and the argument Rome knows best is military conquest. It's not for nothing that our empire is dedicated to Jupiter – symbol: the thunderbolt. We don't really do philosophy.

That didn't mean I was happy about condemning him to death. He was a harmless weirdo as far as I could see. I did my best. I tried to get him off on a holiday pardon, but the crowd weren't having that. (They'd been got at by the priests, that was obvious.) I told them straight that I couldn't see he'd committed a crime.

"Oh, but he has," said the priests. "He's claimed to be the Son of God."

So I was right: it's not really about political ambitions; he's upsetting the religious apple cart. But 'Son of God' is an interesting choice of words. Do you know who else has that title? The emperor, that's who, our noble lord Tiberius. When his adoptive father Augustus died and was deified, that made Tiberius officially 'Dei Filius'. I can't imagine that a wandering preacher from out in the wilds of Galilee knows much about imperial titles, but even so the coincidence made me uneasy. No one gets to set himself up against Rome and survive.

I had him questioned again, but he still wouldn't say where he was from or what he was up to. It was as if he *wanted* to die, or he'd taken some vow not to speak in his own defence. That didn't stop him quibbling with my authority, mind you. And then the priests started up again with their insinuations:

"Anyone who lets this man go is no friend to Caesar."

I knew what they were trying to do. They've threatened before to appeal to the emperor to have me indicted. There was some trouble years ago about temple money being spent on the new aqueduct. Caesar doesn't care; Rome is a world away, and as long as the provinces are quiet, no one's too bothered about how it's achieved. But I can't afford to make enemies either. And I need to be seen to be strong. Rome has to command respect. If the cost is the life of one troublemaker, who lacks the sense to beg for mercy, so be it. Whatever world he thought he was king of, he had to die. That's the truth of it. In the end, I had the power. He only had words, and what good are those?

16

A Terrible Mistake

The Death of Judas
by Matthew

MATTHEW 27:1-10

Judas, my friend, what have you done? You were always the planner, the organiser, the one who saw the destination and then worked out how we would get there. You weren't interested in who was in or out of the inner circle, and you rarely troubled the teacher with questions. You took care of the money, stashing it away in the good days and eking it out in the thinner times, so somehow or other we always had enough to get by on. If it hadn't been for you and me, imagine how those fishermen would have squandered it. Some of them can hardly count their own fish. Being a tax collector all those years might have given me pariah status, but at least it taught me the value of coins in the pocket. And you had just the right combination of steeliness and vision. No one was going to sweet-talk you into spending unnecessarily, if it put the teacher's plan in jeopardy. Even when he authorised it himself, in one of his rare moments of extravagance, I remember you sighing over the waste. I know John thinks you had your hand in the bag but I've never seen any evidence of it, nothing you've bought for yourself or handed over to your family. Anyway, the teacher trusted you to look after the money, and that's enough for me.

Sometimes it seemed he trusted you with other things as well. We've seen you talking to him alone, heartfelt conversations we couldn't quite overhear: you gesticulating and raising your voice, him always patient, not conceding, but gentle. And that last meal which none of us understood until it was too late, when it seemed as if the two of you were talking in some kind of code, as if you knew what was going on but the rest of us were in the dark.

A Terrible Mistake

I know how frustrated you were sometimes, by the way he resolutely turned his face away from power. Every time there was a chance to get into a position of influence, he somehow melted away into the background. You thought it was his blind spot – I remember you sitting with Simon for hours quizzing him about the zealots and their strategies. How can a small number of dedicated people optimise their power to create a force for good? But lately it seemed you realised that no army we could raise was going to have an impact on the Romans. Once we'd got to Jerusalem, and he'd started to debate with the Pharisees in earnest, it became obvious that that was his secret weapon. No one could touch him in rhetoric. He knew the Scriptures as if he'd written them himself, and he had that wonderfully deft touch, which could turn from humour to anecdote to a killer put-down from one sentence to the next.

I think that's when the idea came to you: he needed to be on a larger stage, where not just the pilgrims but all the world could hear him. Then people would open their hearts to him, because who could fail to respond to that combination of certainty, fearlessness and compassion? He'd be invincible, generating a momentum that nothing in the world could halt. It's like Job says to God himself: "I know that you can do all things; no purpose of yours can be thwarted."

I'll say this for you, Judas, you always saw the big picture. Except your big picture wasn't quite in line with his, was it? Did you agree it with him? Did you know his plan? Of course, we all heard him say it: "The Son of Man will be delivered over to the chief priests and be condemned to death." But we didn't want to know, or we thought he was talking in parables again. Did you understand? Is that why you were whispering together at the end of the meal? It looked as if he was sending you off somewhere; I thought I heard him say, "Go quickly, and do what you need to do." We all know how that ended: with the armed men in the garden, and your face in the torchlight, brushing against his. But I can't believe that you wanted it to turn out the way it did.

I think you were so convinced by his brilliance that you wanted him to be put on trial, because you knew that he would wipe the floor with any advocates they put up against him. You hadn't reckoned with the fickleness of the crowd, the poisoned menace of the chief priests, or his sudden refusal to defend himself. It was like a repeat of the Galilee days when people wanted to crown him king but he couldn't be found; here was his biggest opportunity yet to get his message across, and he wouldn't take it. The greatest orator of our time was silent in his own defence, and so they found him guilty on a trumped up charge.

There's so much pain and shame in my mind about that night that I'm still trying to make sense of it. We were terrified, and aghast; we knew we'd let him down, but how were we to know that he would willingly cooperate in his own destruction? None of us saw that, Judas, but it must have hit you hardest of all. I saw you throw back the money they paid you, the coins bouncing over the temple courtyard. I ran after you and tried to speak to you, but you were past reasoning with by then. "He told me to do it!" was all you would say.

So I come sometimes to sit here, in the Potter's Field, where they're making a little cemetery for foreigners, and say some of the things I wish I'd been able to say to you before. You're right: he did tell you to do it. He knew – most of the time – what was in all our minds, and he must have known what was in yours. He let you betray him, Judas. It was part of his plan. I know you'd say that it doesn't take away your guilt; you chose to bring the guards, to precipitate that travesty of a trial. But you know, we all failed him when it came to it. You should have seen Peter; he was a wreck of a man. And you know now that that terrible night, and the terrible day that followed, weren't the end. Death was too small to hold him. The power of his speech was channelled into the strength of his silence, and that power exploded through the gates of hell and burst back into life. We knew there was no one like him, but we had no idea how far beyond our imagining he was. Afterwards, meeting him again was terrifying – and yet like coming home. He had a kind of majesty to him that made it hard to look at him straight, but he was as generous as ever. He forgave us all, even Peter, who's still having difficulty forgiving himself. He would have forgiven you, Judas, if you'd only waited to give him the chance.

17

The Light Returns

Resurrection

by Mary Magdalene

JOHN 20:1-18

Even in the worst times, I've never known darkness like this. It's not just absence of light; it's the opposite of light, as if the sun had been sucked out of the sky by a force stronger than life itself. And yet the sun still rises, and I am still alive, even though all I wish for is to die. I know what it is to be lost, but this is like being cast adrift on a shoreless sea. Because someone found me, and rescued me, and now he's gone; and all the blessed, beautiful things of life – hope, truth, love, joy – are gone with him, into a black void from which nothing can escape.

There is still one thing I have to do, one last, useless gesture. On that unthinkable day there was no time for anointing before night fell for the Sabbath. All yesterday the unfinished task clawed at me, but now leaving the house feels like a physical pain. It's only bearable because, this early, the sky too is dark. Even so, I keep to the back streets and the shadows. The tomb is in a lonely place, on the edge of the city, outside the walls where the demons are supposed to live – but that doesn't scare me now. I know what demons can do. I've lived in the shadow of fear and anger and pain, twisting together like a noose around my mind, crushing me into hopelessness or goading me into fury. Then the man who came to us from God set me free, gave me a vision of a life I could never have imagined, full of richness and wonder and peace. But now God's anointed one is dead, the demons are coming for us all.

Because it's so dark, it's not until I'm almost at the tomb entrance that I realise something has changed. The great stone they rolled across its mouth has gone. For a moment, I think I must have mistaken the place. But I recognise the olive tree just opposite, leaning away as if in disbelief.

And here is a broken jar of ointment that we must have dropped two days ago in our haste and grief. What new horror is this? Have they desecrated the grave? The soldiers didn't want to let us bury him; by their rules, criminals don't get tombs. Instead there's a stinking gully behind Golgotha where the corpses get flung for the wild dogs to eat. It was only thanks to one of the Sanhedrin, a man with money and the ear of the Governor, that we were allowed to take his body away – and only then because he hinted there might be violence during Passover otherwise. It was a good, brave act from someone who'd have been better advised to keep his head down. Was it all for nothing? Did the authorities just wait till everyone was busy with the festival and steal the body anyway? Desolation spikes me like a sword thrust. Will they take even this away, my final, futile gift to the man who gave me back my life? I wanted to anoint his cold body with the honour it was denied in death. I wanted to make him fragrant with spices, as he made my life fragrant with meaning, but I cannot.

I daren't stay here. What to do? Who to trust? I think of the twelve. They were useless at the arrest, and too scared to show their faces at the trial; but we're all useless now. I know where Peter's staying, not far away, and I must tell someone.

When I find his house, it takes a while to rouse him and get him to understand, but then he has to see for himself. He grabs a friend and they run back to the tomb together, through the grey dawn. I follow them, but they're faster than me, so I arrive to see Peter coming out of the tomb entrance, shaking his head in puzzlement. He isn't even trying to be discreet. Lucky for him, there's no sign of the soldiers, or we'd all be taken in for questioning. It still isn't safe to be a follower, even now it's all over. The two of them search, but there's no trace of the body, not even a mark where it's been dragged away. They've left the wrappings, though. Somehow, that makes it worse. In death they took away even the dignity of his covering. The thought of his tortured body, exposed for all to see, takes me back to the dreadful, suffocating hours of the execution. Is it my imagination, or do I hear the demons cackling?

Peter is anxious to find the others, tell them this latest, crushing news. Now it's too late, he's full of action. But I feel the dark descending again. Something draws me to the tomb, with all its horror. It's the last place I saw him, his strong body so heartbreakingly fragile, the blood congealing on his mangled feet. When the men have gone, I sit down by the gaping entrance, hoping for – what? That somehow the stones might be imprinted with a memory of his precious, life-affirming love? I think how he had love enough for us all, for impetuous Peter, impractical John, high-born Joanna, fastidious Martha, and me. I weep at the waste – such love, overflowing and freely given. Where is it now? Where did it go to when they broke his body and banished his spirit?

"Woman," says a voice, "why are you weeping?"

I flinch, but it's not a soldier. It comes from the tomb. Cautiously, I peer inside. In the dawn light I make out two figures, dressed in white. I have no idea who they are, but now I am past caring.

"They have taken away my Lord," I say, and the words bring home to me the force of my loss. "I do not know where they have laid him."

I don't wait for a reply. Wherever his spirit has gone, it's not here in the tomb. This is a place of emptiness, an end, not a beginning. Perhaps, after all, I can find solace with the disciples. His mother will be good to me. I know that she too is speared by grief, but she has an unshakeable core of kindness, and she knows what it is to have loved him without measure. At least we have that in common.

As I turn to leave, the sun slips over the horizon of the hills, and I'm momentarily dazzled. Silhouetted against the light is the figure of another man, only a few yards from the tomb. He's not a soldier either; he carries no weapon. Nor a demon; he speaks gently, asking me what I'm looking for. A gardener, then, come to tend the trees? Perhaps he knows where I might find the body. Abandoning caution, I simply ask him. There is a pause, and then he says my name: "Mary."

Recognition washes over me like a wave, and I want to drown myself in it. It is him, gloriously alive, clothed in the majesty of the morning. His voice speaks as if out of my dreams. It has all its familiar compassion and strength, but there's something new too: a note of joy and freedom. I stretch my hands out towards him, but he stays out of reach.

"You must not hold on to me now," he says. "I am going to my father, who is your father too. But I have a task for you, Mary. You must be my witness. Go to my brothers and tell them what you have heard and seen."

And then he is gone, leaving me alone with the new day. So it was just a hallucination, then, a cruel trick of the demons. I brace myself for the tide of hopelessness rolling back in to claim me, but it doesn't come. Instead I feel a lightness and ease, as if I've waded out of a river into clear air. In the olive tree a bird starts to sing, a paean of praise for this beautiful day, filling the morning with music and light. I feel as if I am alive on the first day of creation, watching the world spring forth from a great well of love and joy. His life quivers around me, even though I can no longer see him. When he spoke my name, something took root inside me, a secret so precious and powerful that nothing can overcome it, not soldiers, or demons, or death itself. Nor ridicule. "Tell my brothers," he said, and I almost laugh at the absurdity. I'll tell them, and they won't believe a word of it. Even without my history, who would accept the evidence of a woman for such a ridiculous, impossible story?

But then I think, isn't it just like him to entrust this most extraordinary news to someone whose testimony has no legal status? He was always one to turn convention upside down. He proclaimed the kingdom of heaven in fields and roadsides for peasants and petty criminals to hear. He welcomed children and turned his back on the powerful. He met hatred with kindness and hostility with compassion. And now, in the biggest reversal of all, he has gone through the gates of death and returned, so full of life that it spills out on everything around him. The grass springs green where he walked, the air tastes sweet as perfume, and the colours stand out with a sharpness that's almost painful. The grey emptiness that swirled in my head has gone. It's as if the life and love that blaze out of him have filled me up, and left no space for despair and weakness. I don't begin to understand what's just happened, but something has changed, and my world will never be the same again.

18

God With Us

Apocalypse

by a disciple

LUKE 19:41-44; 21:20-36

I'm old now. Old, and slow, and perhaps a bit forgetful – and I can see the end of my life approaching. And after that, who knows – received into Abraham's bosom, or the cold darkness of Sheol? The rabbis disagree; and the prophecies – as always – provide as many different answers as there are questions. I hope there is some kind of resolution, because who doesn't want to think that there will be some eternal explanation to make sense of all the problems of life?

It's true what they say: it's no fun being old. Your body starts to disobey you – your limbs slow to move and creaking like rotting timber. Or else your wits go wandering, marooning you in a world where no one can reach you and nothing makes sense. And even if your mind is still sharp, all that knowledge and experience you've amassed counts for nothing. The young don't respect their elders these days; they always know best, with their shiny new enthusiasms and their excitable plans for turning the world upside down. They don't want to hear from people who've seen it all before.

To tell the truth, I'm not sure I was any different when I was young. I didn't want to be told either. I was as full of fervour as any zealot, drunk with the possibilities of life stretching ahead of me. We thought we were building the kingdom of God on earth. Impossible to believe that I'd end up like this – where just getting to be old counts as an achievement. We thought our lives were charmed, that we would live for ever, or at least for long enough to become legends. When I think of all my friends, lost, enslaved, slaughtered, I wonder why I was the one to survive. And why did we not see it coming?

Seeing the Light

He told us, of course, the teacher, but we didn't hear him. It's odd how in my old age some of the events from years ago seem closer than what happened yesterday. But then, didn't he tell us, "Heaven and earth will pass away, but my words will never pass away"? I can remember him saying it, how the words struck dread into our hearts even as we were trying to jolly him out of his despondency. He was like that: so full of passion and possibility one moment, prophesying doom the next. No one wanted to hear the doom bits. Not Peter, who was shipped off to Rome, never to be heard of again. Not James, put to death by Herod. Not the rest of the inner circle, imprisoned, tortured and then scattered far and wide by the persecution. And not the hundreds of hangers-on who were caught up in the revolt and the cataclysm that followed.

I wonder if you can imagine an apocalypse. The best way I can describe it is that the world just stops making sense – like an earthquake turning solid ground to liquid, or a volcanic eruption where the air you breathe is transformed to suffocating dust. It was never ideal living under Roman occupation, but we didn't know how lucky we were. We thought they'd done their worst – that our God would preserve us from their attacks. We had no idea. When the rebellion came, we held them off for a few brief months and thought we were heroes. They just sent bigger armies and better generals. We thought they'd ruled harshly before, but there was no comparison. Can you picture a whole city slowly starving to death? Do you know how plague rips through a captive population when the water supply starts to run out? Have you seen what a Roman army on the rampage can do? It was a slow suffocation, followed by a rout, followed by a massacre. They were utterly without mercy. The old, the ill, the children, all butchered. The ones they thought might be useful, chained and branded for slavery, or sent to the arena to die a different kind of death for public amusement. Where was our God then? Why did he turn his back on us?

Oh, we know the score. If we don't listen to God, if we break our side of the covenant, he is no longer bound to protect us. But truthfully, were we any worse than previous generations? Why did the wrath of the ages come to land on us? And what of the teacher's talk of a new world of favour towards God's people? I don't have the answers to that. Truthfully, I hardly know how to go on believing in the God of Israel, when Israel is laid waste and her people are scattered, enslaved, subjugated. I'd like to give up on God altogether. But then I remember the teacher, who had his own appointment with doom. He knew what it meant to be trapped, suffocating in a long, slow agony, then spitted with a spear at the end. You can't say he didn't share in the suffering.

And then what? I know I'm an old man, and you'll think I'm foolish and forgetful, but I know what I saw. I was there when he came back. He died and was buried; there are plenty of witnesses to that, not least the Romans who – I think we can say – know a thing or two about killing. And then he wasn't dead any more. Death couldn't hold him down. Suffering couldn't destroy him. He was changed, but also the same, still as enigmatic as ever, but his talk was about repentance and forgiveness, not vengeance on his enemies, or ours either, come to that. He reminded us that if we followed him we would suffer – though I don't think any of us understood what that would mean. Suffering always looks easier from the outside. When it happens to you, it's in real time, with pain that you can't escape – and always the sense of outrage: How can this be happening to me? Why doesn't God make it stop? For answer we have only God's reply to Job: "Where were you when I laid the earth's foundation? Who has a claim against me that I must pay? Everything under heaven belongs to me."

If everything belongs to God, that means suffering belongs to him too – and even death, I suppose. For so long we've been told suffering is his punishment for our wrongdoing – and heaven knows, in my lifetime I've seen enough examples of people's selfishness and arrogance causing suffering to others. We imagined that if we tried very hard to be obedient we could live without pain, in a perpetual golden glow of God's approval. Worse, when God showered us with prosperity and peace, we took it for a sign that we had earned his favour, not a generous gift. I remember the teacher: he loved his food and was always up for a party. But he never hung on to the good times, or reminisced about how much better his reception had been in Galilee. He was no stoic; he felt pain with the rest of us, and I've seen him in tears from frustration or longing or grief. But he didn't run away from suffering like most people do. His secret, if he had one, was that he knew how to trust in God even through his suffering – as if suffering were just another route to God.

I wouldn't say that living through the destruction of Jerusalem has brought me to God. I don't have the teacher's vision, or his holiness. What I'm left with is grief, and a terrifying sense of my own mortality. When you've seen a child die of starvation before your eyes, or hidden behind a wall and heard a legionary butchering a fugitive, you realise you're only one heartbeat away from death yourself. A human life is a grain of sand in God's sight. It won't be long now before mine is over. But I hold on to the teacher's sayings: "the one who stands firm to the end shall be saved". There are those who say we should endure hardship as discipline – as the Lord's way of teaching us to be better. But to me its meaning goes deeper than that: it reminds us that God is everywhere, in the deepest reaches of the sea, in the highest mountains, in the depths of our despair. There is nowhere we can go where we are out of God's protection. It's true what the psalm says: "If I go up to the heavens, you are there; if I make my bed in the depths, you are there." Suffering is agony, there's no getting round that. But God is not absent, even in the worst of it. He came to live alongside us – that's what we were so slow to understand. We didn't recognise him, because our minds were still fixed on the God of thunder and judgement. He taught us and healed us, but what seems most precious to me now is that he shared our human frailty. He experienced pain and hunger and hopelessness, to show us in the clearest way possible that we are never alone in our suffering. And then he faced down hell itself and came through triumphant. So I do what I can to keep living as he taught us: looking out for those who have even less than I do, noticing God's small gifts when a bird sings or a seed sprouts in the dust. And I hold on to the hope that when my time comes, whatever death brings, he will be there too.

Contact the Author

To contact the author, please write to:

Ruth Carter
c/o Onwards and Upwards Publishers Ltd.
4 The Old Smithy
London Road
Rockbeare
EX5 2EA

More information about the author can be found on the book's web page:

www.onwardsandupwards.org/seeing-the-light

Similar Books from the Publisher

The Little Blog of Lucanus
Simon Ratsey
ISBN: 978-1-911086-84-0

The Apostle Paul's missionary journeys are vividly portrayed in this imagined yet fact-filled diary of Doctor Luke, the writer of the Book of Acts. Based on the Bible's narrative and filled with cultural and historical background, Luke describes how it feels to travel by land and sea across the Roman Empire, bringing the Good News of Jesus to diverse communities, and experiencing the joys of seeing lives changed and the challenges of persecution and opposition.

Simply Stories of Jesus
Dorothy Wigan
ISBN: 978-1-911086-80-2

Dorothy Wigan brings events from the ministry of Jesus to life in a fresh way, retelling the stories from the perspective of those whose lives were transformed through their encounters with him.

Books available from all good bookshops and from the publisher:

www.onwardsandupwards.org/shop